Table of Conten

Table of Contents *continued*

Table of Contents *continued*

Introduction

The National Council of Teachers of English and the International Reading Association prepared standards for the English language arts. These standards "grew out of current research and theory about how students learn—in particular, how they learn language." These standards address "what students should know and be able to do in the English language arts."

One standard is that students should be able to communicate effectively by learning the "language of wider communication," the forms of the English language that are most commonly identified as standard English. Students must recognize the importance of audience when they write and speak so they will be able to use the appropriate form of language for the intended audience. The standards acknowledge that "students need guidance and practice to develop their skills in academic writing. . . . They need to understand the varying demands of different kinds of writing tasks and to recognize how to adapt tone, style, and content for the particular task at hand." Again, students must "consider the needs of their audiences as they compose, edit, and revise."

Another standard emphasizes that "students apply knowledge of language structure, language conventions. . . ." Students need practice with accepted language conventions (e.g., capitalization, punctuation, grammar) in order to develop awareness and consistent application in their writing.

Language Practice is a program designed for students who require additional practice in the basics of effective writing and speaking. Focused practice in key grammar, usage, mechanics, and composition areas helps students gain ownership of essential skills. The logical sequence of the practice exercises, combined with a clear and concise format, allows for easy and independent use.

National Council of Teachers of English and International Reading Association, *Standards for the English Language Arts*, 1996.

Organization

Language Practice provides systematic, focused attention to just one carefully selected skill at a time. Rules are clearly stated at the beginning of each lesson. Key terms are introduced in bold type. The rules are then illustrated with examples and followed by meaningful practice exercises.

Lessons are organized around a series of units. They are arranged in a logical sequence beginning with vocabulary; progressing through sentences, grammar and usage, and mechanics; and culminating with composition skills.

Grades 3 through 8 include a final unit on study skills, which can be assigned as needed. This unit includes such skills as organizing information, following directions, using a dictionary, using the library, and choosing appropriate reference sources.

Skills are reviewed thoroughly in a two-page test at the conclusion of each unit. These unit tests are presented in a standardized test format. The content of each unit is repeated and expanded in subsequent levels as highlighted in the skills correlation chart on pages 6 and 7.

Use

Throughout the program, *Language Practice* stresses the application of language principles. In addition to matching, circling, or underlining elements in a predetermined sentence, lessons ask students to use what they have learned in an original sentence or in rewriting a sentence.

Language Practice is designed for independent use by students who have had instruction in the specific skills covered in these lessons. Copies of the activities can be given to individuals, pairs of students, or small groups for completion. They can also be used as a center activity. If students are familiar with the content, the worksheets can be homework for reviewing and reinforcing skills.

From the beginning, students feel comfortable with the format of the lessons. Each lesson is introduced with a rule at the top of the page and ends with a meaningful exercise at the bottom of the page. Each lesson is clearly labeled, and directions are clear and uncomplicated. Because the format is logical and consistent and the vocabulary is carefully controlled, most students can use *Language Practice* with a high degree of independence. As the teacher, this allows you the time needed to help students on a one-to-one basis.

Special Feature

The process approach to teaching writing provides success for most students. *Language Practice* provides direct support for the teaching of composition and significantly enhances those strategies and techniques commonly associated with the process-writing approach.

Each book includes a composition unit that provides substantial work with important composition skills, such as considering audience, writing topic sentences, selecting supporting details, taking notes, writing reports, and revising and proofreading. Also included in the composition unit is practice with various prewriting activities, such as clustering and brainstorming, which play an important role in process writing. The composition lessons are presented in the same rule-plus-practice format as in other units.

Additional Notes

- Parent Communication. Sign the *Letter to Parents* and send it home with the students. This letter offers suggestions for parental involvement to increase learner success.

- Assessment Test. Use the Assessment Test on pages 8 through 11 to determine the skills your students need to practice.

- Language Terms. Provide each student with a copy of the list of language terms on page 12 to keep for reference throughout the year. Also place a copy in the classroom language arts center for reference.

- Center Activities. Use the worksheets as center activities to give students the opportunity to work cooperatively.

- Have fun. The activities use a variety of strategies to maintain student interest. Watch your students' language improve as skills are applied in structured, relevant practice!

Dear Parent,

During this school year, our class will be working with a language program that covers the basics of effective writing and speaking. To increase your child's language skills, we will be completing activity sheets that provide practice to ensure mastery of these important skills.

From time to time, I may send home activity sheets. To best help your child, please consider the following suggestions:

- Provide a quiet place to work.
- Go over the rules, examples, and directions together.
- Encourage your child to do his or her best.
- Check the lesson when it is complete.
- Go over your child's work, and note improvements as well as concerns.

Help your child maintain a positive attitude about language skills. Let your child know that each lesson provides an opportunity to have fun and to learn. If your child expresses anxiety about these skills, help him or her understand what causes the stress. Then talk about ways to deal with it in a positive way.

Above all, enjoy this time you spend with your child. He or she will feel your support, and skills will improve with each activity completed.

Thank you for your help!

Cordially,

Skills Correlation

	1	2	3	4	5	6	7	8
Vocabulary								
Sound Words (Onomatopoeia)	■							
Rhyming Words	■	■						
Synonyms	■	■	■	■	■	■	■	■
Antonyms	■	■	■	■	■	■	■	■
Homonyms	■	■	■	■	■	■	■	■
Multiple Meanings/Homographs	■	■		■	■	■	■	■
Prefixes and Suffixes			■	■	■	■	■	■
Base and Root Words			■	■	■	■	■	■
Compound Words			■	■	■	■	■	■
Contractions			■	■	■	■	■	■
Idioms						■	■	■
Connotation/Denotation						■	■	■
Sentences								
Word Order in Sentences	■	■						
Recognizing a Sentence	■	■	■	■	■	■	■	■
Subjects and Predicates	■	■	■	■	■	■	■	■
Types of Sentences	■	■	■	■	■	■	■	■
Compound/Complex Sentences			■	■	■	■	■	■
Sentence Combining			■	■	■	■	■	■
Run-On Sentences				■	■	■	■	■
Independent and Subordinate Clauses							■	■
Compound Subjects and Predicates						■	■	■
Direct and Indirect Objects							■	■
Inverted Word Order						■	■	■
Grammar and Usage								
Common and Proper Nouns	■	■	■	■	■	■	■	■
Singular and Plural Nouns	■	■	■	■	■	■	■	■
Possessive Nouns			■	■	■	■	■	■
Appositives						■	■	■
Verbs	■	■	■	■	■	■	■	■
Verb Tense	■	■	■	■	■	■	■	■
Regular/Irregular Verbs	■	■	■	■	■	■	■	■
Subject/Verb Agreement		■	■	■	■	■	■	■
Verb Phrases						■	■	■
Transitive and Intransitive Verbs							■	■
Verbals: Gerunds, Participles, and Infinitives							■	■
Active and Passive Voice							■	■
Mood								■
Pronouns	■	■	■	■	■	■	■	■
Antecedents							■	■
Articles	■	■	■					
Adjectives	■	■	■	■	■	■	■	■
Correct Word Usage (e.g. *may/can, sit/set*)	■	■	■		■	■	■	■
Adverbs			■	■	■	■	■	■
Prepositions						■	■	■
Prepositional Phrases						■	■	■
Conjunctions						■	■	■
Interjections						■	■	■
Double Negatives								■
Capitalization and Punctuation								
Capitalization: First Word in Sentence	■	■	■	■	■	■	■	
Capitalization: Proper Nouns	■	■	■	■	■	■	■	■
Capitalization: in Letters		■	■	■	■	■	■	■

Capitalization and Punctuation (cont'd)	1	2	3	4	5	6	7	8
Capitalization: Abbreviations		■	■	■	■	■	■	■
Capitalization: Titles		■	■	■	■	■	■	■
Capitalization: Proper Adjectives						■	■	■
End Punctuation	■	■	■	■	■	■	■	■
Commas		■	■	■	■	■	■	■
Apostrophes in Contractions		■	■	■	■	■	■	■
Apostrophes in Possessives			■	■	■	■	■	■
Quotation Marks			■	■	■	■	■	■
Colons/Semicolons						■	■	■
Hyphens						■	■	■
Composition								
Expanding Sentences					■	■	■	■
Writing a Paragraph		■	■	■	■	■	■	■
Paragraphs: Topic Sentence (main idea)		■	■	■	■	■	■	■
Paragraphs: Supporting Details		■	■	■	■	■	■	■
Order In Paragraphs		■	■	■	■	■	■	
Writing Process:								
Establishing Purpose		■		■		■	■	■
Audience						■	■	■
Topic		■		■	■	■	■	■
Outlining				■		■	■	■
Clustering/Brainstorming						■	■	
Notetaking						■	■	
Revising/Proofreading						■	■	■
Types of Writing:								
Letter	■	■	■			■		
"How-to" Paragraph			■					
Invitation			■					
Telephone Message			■					
Conversation				■				
Narrative Paragraph				■				
Comparing and Contrasting					■			
Descriptive Paragraph					■			
Report						■		
Interview							■	
Persuasive Composition								■
Readiness/Study Skills								
Grouping	■							
Letters of Alphabet	■							
Listening	■	■						
Making Comparisons	■	■						
Organizing Information	■	■	■					
Following Directions	■	■	■	■	■			
Alphabetical Order	■	■	■	■	■	■	■	■
Using a Dictionary:								
Definitions		■	■	■	■	■	■	■
Guide Words/Entry Words		■	■	■	■	■	■	■
Syllables			■	■	■	■	■	■
Multiple Meanings						■	■	■
Word Origins						■	■	■
Parts of a Book						■	■	■
Using the Library						■	■	■
Using Encyclopedias				■	■	■	■	■
Using Reference Books						■	■	■
Using the *Readers' Guide*							■	■
Choosing Appropriate Sources						■	■	■

Name _____   Date _____

Assessment Test

A. Write <u>S</u> before each pair of synonyms, <u>A</u> before each pair of antonyms, and <u>H</u> before each pair of homonyms.

_____ **1.** board, bored   _____ **3.** antique, ancient

_____ **2.** tall, short   _____ **4.** massive, huge

B. Write the homograph for the pair of meanings.

_____ **a.** a piece of hair   **b.** to fasten securely

C. Write <u>P</u> before each word with a prefix, <u>S</u> before each word with a suffix, and <u>C</u> before each compound word.

_____ **1.** overcome   _____ **3.** rusty

_____ **2.** misplace   _____ **4.** disinterested

D. Write the words that make up each contraction.

_____ **1.** they'll   _____ **2.** we've

E. Underline the word in parentheses that has the more positive connotation.

The (crabby, unhappy) child squirmed in her mother's arms.

F. Circle the number of the idiom that means <u>to suddenly become angry</u>.

1. put up with   **2.** fly off the handle

G. Write <u>D</u> before the declarative sentence, <u>IM</u> before the imperative sentence, <u>E</u> before the exclamatory sentence, and <u>IN</u> before the interrogative sentence. Then underline the simple subject, and circle the simple predicate in each sentence.

_____ **1.** Wait until the speech is over.   _____ **3.** Ouch! I burned myself!

_____ **2.** What do you believe?   _____ **4.** That article really made me angry.

H. Write <u>CS</u> before the sentence that has a compound subject and <u>CP</u> before the sentence that has a compound predicate.

_____ **1.** He stumbled and fell on the rough ground.

_____ **2.** Carmen and José are the leading actors.

I. Write <u>CS</u> before the compound sentence. Write <u>RO</u> before the run-on sentence. Write <u>I</u> before the sentence that is in inverted order.

_____ **1.** Through the woods ran the frightened deer.

_____ **2.** Once she had lived in New York, she lives in Toronto now.

_____ **3.** Brenda was cold, so she built a roaring fire.

J. Put brackets around the subordinate clause, and underline the independent clause in this complex sentence. Then write <u>DO</u> above the direct object.

Before I left, I ate a good breakfast.

K. Underline the common nouns, and circle the proper nouns in the sentence.

Mayor Dumonte showed the citizens of our city that he was honest by appointing Ms. Lopez to the position.

L. Circle the appositive in the sentence. Underline the noun it identifies or explains.

His favorite nurse, Ms. Abram, made his stay in the hospital more pleasant.

M. Write <u>past</u>, <u>present</u>, or <u>future</u> to show the tense of each underlined verb.

_____ **1.** We <u>will have</u> the best seats in the house.

_____ **2.** The actors <u>prepare</u> for months beforehand.

_____ **3.** Critics <u>described</u> this play as one of the best ever.

N. Circle the correct verbs in each sentence.

1. Here (is, are) the paper clips you (were, was) asking for.

2. She (seen, saw) her brother before he (know, knew) she was there.

3. It had (begun, began) to rain, so he (gone, went) inside.

4. She (thrown, threw) the dish and (broken, broke) it.

O. Circle the number of the sentence that is in the active voice.

1. The letter was received a day late.

2. Jerry sent his package in overnight mail.

P. Write <u>SP</u> before the sentence that has a subject pronoun, **OP** before the sentence that has an object pronoun, **PP** before the sentence that has a possessive pronoun, and **IP** before the sentence that has an indefinite pronoun. Circle the pronoun in each sentence.

_____ **1.** Somebody knows what happened.   _____ **3.** The band played their favorite song.

_____ **2.** Rick wrote that poem for her.   _____ **4.** We felt surprised and upset.

Q. Underline the pronoun. Circle its antecedent.

The jets flew in their assigned formation.

R. On the line before each sentence, write <u>adjective</u> or <u>adverb</u> to describe the underlined word.

_____ **1.** <u>That</u> farm is up for sale.

_____ **2.** The dog's yelps were <u>extremely</u> loud.

_____ **3.** She spoke <u>more enthusiastically</u> than anyone else.

_____ **4.** Some <u>Mexican</u> food is very spicy and hot.

S. Underline each prepositional phrase twice. Circle each preposition. Underline the conjunction once.

The girl on the bus waved at me while it passed by.

T. Rewrite the letter. Add capital letters and punctuation where needed.

956 e. garden circle
bowman tx 78787
april 13 19___

dear steve

    were so excited youre coming to visit ___ even little scott managed to say uncle steve visit which was pretty good for a child of only twenty two months wouldnt you agree ___ oh i want to be sure i have the information correct ___ please let me know as soon as possible if any of this is wrong flight 561 arrives at 310 P.M. on may 22 ___ see you then ___

your sister
amanda

_____

_____

_____

_____

_____

_____

_____

_____

_____

_____

_____

U. Number the sentences in order, with the topic sentence first.

_____ **1.** Then the wool is combed and formed into neat rolls.

_____ **2.** Making wool thread by hand is a time-consuming art.

_____ **3.** The spinner goes to work making thread after the wool is combed.

_____ **4.** First, a sheep's wool is shaved off and cleaned.

V. Circle the number of the best interview question.

1. Is it your feeling that the city council's decision has failed the voters?

2. Why do you think that the mayor voted against the rest of the council?

W. Rewrite the sentence below. Correct the errors in the sentence by following the proofreader's marks.

Although ∧the decision to t̶o̶ close mayfield park was unpoplar, proved it to be the correct choise⊙

_____

X. Use the dictionary entry to answer the questions.

jolly (jäl′ ē) *adj.* **1.** full of high spirits: joyous. **2.** expressing, suggesting, or inspiring gaiety: cheerful. [Middle English *joli.*]

1. What part of speech is the word jolly? _____

2. Would jolly come before or after joust in the dictionary? _____

3. Which language is in the history of the word jolly? _____

4. Write jolly separated into syllables. _____

Y. Write the source from the box that you would use to find the information listed.

dictionary	card catalog	encyclopedia	atlas	*Readers' Guide*

_____ **1.** where to find an article in a certain magazine

_____ **2.** where to locate a certain book

_____ **3.** a map of Europe

_____ **4.** the etymology of the word lieutenant

_____ **5.** an article on soapstone

Z. Use the encyclopedia sample to answer the questions.

CREE is the name of a Native American people now living on reservations in Canada. They were originally forest hunters and trappers who traded with the early French and English fur traders. Part of the group moved southwest into buffalo country and became known as Plains Cree. *See also* NATIVE AMERICANS.

1. What is the article about? _____

2. Where did some members of the tribe move? _____

3. Under what subject heading can you find related information? _____

Language Terms

action verb a verb that expresses action

active voice a sentence in which the subject acts

adjective modifies a noun by telling which one, what kind, or how many

adverb modifies a verb, an adjective, or another adverb

antecedent the word to which a pronoun refers

antonym has the opposite meaning of another word

apostrophe a mark used to show where a letter or letters have been left out of a contraction

appositive a noun or phrase that identifies or explains the noun it follows

clause a group of words that contains a subject and a predicate

common noun names any one of a class of objects

complete predicate the part of a sentence that includes all the words that state action or condition of the subject

complete subject the part of a sentence that includes all the words that tell who or what the sentence is about

complex sentence contains one independent clause and one or more subordinate clauses

compound predicate two or more simple predicates

compound sentence two or more independent clauses

compound subject two or more simple subjects

compound word a word made up of two or more words

conjunction a word used to join words or groups of words

connotation suggests something positive or negative

contraction a word formed by joining two other words

declarative sentence a sentence that makes a statement

demonstrative adjective points out a specific person or thing

denotation the exact meaning of a word

direct object who or what receives the action of the verb

exclamatory sentence expresses strong emotion

gerund a verb form ending in -ing used as a noun

helping verb used to help the main verb of the sentence

homograph has the same spelling as another word, but a different meaning and sometimes a different pronunciation

homonym sounds like another word, but has a different meaning and is spelled differently

idiom an expression that has a meaning different from the usual meanings of the individual words within it

imperative sentence expresses a command or a request

indefinite pronoun does not refer to a specific person or thing

independent clause a clause that can stand alone as a sentence because it expresses a complete thought

indirect object tells to whom or for whom an action is done

infinitive the base form of the verb, usually preceded by to

interrogative sentence a sentence that asks a question

intransitive verb does not need an object

inverted order the order of a sentence when all or part of the predicate comes before the subject

limiting adjective the articles a, an, and the

linking verb a verb that links the subject to a word that either describes the subject or gives the subject another name

natural order the order of a sentence when the subject comes before all or part of the predicate

noun a word that names a person, place, thing, or quality

object of the preposition noun or pronoun in the prepositional phrase

object pronoun used after an action verb or preposition

participle a present or past tense verb used as an adjective

passive voice a sentence in which the subject receives the action

phrase a group of closely related words used as a single part of speech but not containing a subject and predicate

possessive noun shows possession of the noun that follows

possessive pronoun used to show ownership

predicate the part of a sentence that tells what the subject does or what happens to the subject

prefix a syllable added to the beginning of a base word that changes the meaning of the word

preposition a word that shows the relationship of a noun or a pronoun to another word in the sentence

prepositional phrase a group of words that begins with a preposition and ends with a noun or pronoun

pronoun a word that takes the place of a noun

proper adjective is formed from a proper noun

proper noun a noun that names a particular person, place, or thing and is capitalized

relative pronoun relates an adjective clause to the noun or pronoun that the clause modifies

run-on sentence two or more independent clauses that are run together without correct punctuation

sentence expresses a complete thought

simple predicate the verb in the complete predicate

simple sentence contains only one independent clause

simple subject the main word in the complete subject

subject the part of a sentence that tells who or what the sentence is about

subject pronoun a pronoun used in the subject of a sentence and after a linking verb

subordinate clause has a subject and predicate but is not a sentence because it does not express a complete thought

subordinating conjunction introduces an adverb clause

suffix a syllable added to the end of a base word that changes the meaning of the word

synonym a word that has the same or nearly the same meaning as one or more other words

transitive verb has a direct object

verb a word that expresses action, being, or state of being

verb phrase a main verb and one or more helping verbs

verb tense tells the time of the action or being

verbal a verb form that functions as a noun or adjective

12

Synonyms and Antonyms

> ■ A **synonym** is a word that has the same or nearly the same meaning as one or more other words.   EXAMPLES: reply – answer   talk – speak

A. Write a synonym for each word below.

1. pleasant _____

2. enough _____

3. leave _____

4. inquire _____

5. fearless _____

6. artificial _____

7. famous _____

8. trade _____

9. house _____

10. nation _____

11. difficult _____

12. vacant _____

B. Write four sentences about recycling. In each sentence, use a synonym for the word in parentheses. Underline the synonym.

1. (packaging) _____

2. (waste) _____

3. (landfill) _____

4. (planet) _____

> ■ An **antonym** is a word that has the opposite meaning of another word.
> EXAMPLES: old – new   bad – good

C. Write an antonym for each word below.

1. failure _____

2. absent _____

3. before _____

4. slow _____

5. all _____

6. forget _____

7. love _____

8. no _____

9. friend _____

10. always _____

11. light _____

12. forward _____

D. In each sentence, write an antonym for the word in parentheses that makes sense in the sentence.

1. Thao ran his hand along the (smooth) _____ surface of the wood.

2. He knew he would have to (stop) _____ sanding it.

3. Only after sanding would he be able to (destroy) _____ a table.

4. He would try to (forget) _____ not to sand it too much.

Homonyms

> ■ A **homonym** is a word that sounds the same as another word but has a different spelling and a different meaning.
> EXAMPLES: aisle – I'll – isle   flower – flour

A **Underline the correct homonym(s) in each sentence below.**

1. The (two, too, to) people walked very slowly (passed, past) the house.

2. The children were (two, too, to) tired (two, too, to) talk.

3. Did you (hear, here) that noise?

4. Yes, I (heard, herd) it.

5. I do (knot, not) (know, no) of a person who is (knot, not) ready to help the hungry people of the world.

6. Michelle, you (seam, seem) to have forgotten about (our, hour) plans for the picnic.

7. Who (won, one) the citizenship (medal, meddle) this year?

8. Jim, how much do you (way, weigh)?

9. The night (air, heir) is (sew, so) cool that you will (knead, need) a light jacket.

10. The small plants were set out in orderly (rows, rose).

11. I (knew, new) those (knew, new) shoes would hurt my (feat, feet).

12. Which states lead in the production of (beat, beet) sugar?

13. We did (not, knot) go to the (seen, scene) of the wreck.

14. Sue wore the belt around her (waist, waste).

B. **Write a homonym for each word below.**

1. peace _____	11. sew _____	21. knight _____
2. altar _____	12. break _____	22. hymn _____
3. to _____	13. week _____	23. through _____
4. way _____	14. rein _____	24. grown _____
5. beech _____	15. bare _____	25. wrap _____
6. plain _____	16. scene _____	26. prey _____
7. coarse _____	17. mite _____	27. strait _____
8. seem _____	18. whole _____	28. sole _____
9. knew _____	19. hoarse _____	29. hear _____
10. sale _____	20. fourth _____	30. ware _____

Name _____ Date _____

Homographs

> ■ A **homograph** is a word that has the same spelling as another word but a different meaning and sometimes a different pronunciation.
> EXAMPLE: <u>saw</u>, meaning "have seen," and <u>saw</u>, meaning "a tool used for cutting"

A. Circle the letter for the definition that best defines each underlined homograph.

1. Sara jumped at the <u>bangs</u> of the exploding balloons.

   a. fringe of hair   **b.** loud noises

2. She grabbed a stick to <u>arm</u> herself against the threat.

   a. part of the body   **b.** take up a weapon

3. The dog's <u>bark</u> woke the family.

   a. noise a dog makes   **b.** outside covering on a tree

4. Mix the pancake <u>batter</u> for three minutes.

   a. person at bat   **b.** mixture for cooking

B. Use the homographs in the box to complete the sentences below. Each homograph will be used twice.

1. Pieces of a board game are _____.

   People who are cashiers are _____.

2. A water bird is a _____.

   To lower the head is to _____.

3. A metal container is a _____.

   If you are able, you _____.

4. To get down from something is to _____.

   If something is on fire, it is _____.

duck
alight
can
checkers

C. Write the homograph for each pair of meanings below. The first letter of each word is given for you.

1. **a.** place for horses   **b.** delay   s_____

2. **a.** a metal fastener   **b.** a sound made with fingers   s_____

3. **a.** to crush   **b.** a yellow vegetable   s_____

4. **a.** a bad doctor   **b.** the sound made by a duck   q_____

5. **a.** to strike   **b.** a party fruit drink   p_____

Prefixes

■ A **prefix** added to the beginning of a base word changes the meaning of the word.

EXAMPLE: <u>dis-</u>, meaning "opposite of," + the base word <u>appear</u> = <u>disappear</u>, meaning "the opposite of appear"

EXAMPLES:

prefix	meaning	prefix	meaning
in-	not	re-	again
dis-	not	fore-	before
un-	not	pre-	before
trans-	across	mis-	wrong
		with-	from, against

■ **Write a new word using one of the prefixes listed above. Then write the meaning of the new word.**

	WORD	NEW WORD	MEANING
1.	fair	_____	_____
2.	justice	_____	_____
3.	tell	_____	_____
4.	warn	_____	_____
5.	visible	_____	_____
6.	spell	_____	_____
7.	agree	_____	_____
8.	see	_____	_____
9.	behave	_____	_____
10.	stand	_____	_____
11.	complete	_____	_____
12.	please	_____	_____
13.	drawn	_____	_____
14.	likely	_____	_____
15.	match	_____	_____
16.	clean	_____	_____
17.	understand	_____	_____
18.	correct	_____	_____

Suffixes

- A **suffix** added to the end of a base word changes the meaning of the word.
  EXAMPLE: -less, meaning "without," + the base word <u>worth</u> = <u>worthless</u>, meaning "without worth"

EXAMPLES:	suffix	meaning	suffix	meaning
	-less	without	-ist	one skilled in
	-ish	of the nature of	-tion	art of
	-ous	full of	-ful	full of
	-en	to make	-al	pertaining to
	-hood	state of being	-able	able to be
	-ward	in the direction of	-ible	able to be
	-ness	quality of		

- Sometimes you need to change the spelling of a base word when a suffix is added.
  EXAMPLE: happy – happiness

- **Write a new word using one of the suffixes listed above. Then write the meaning of the new word.**

	WORD	NEW WORD	MEANING
1.	care	_____	_____
2.	truth	_____	_____
3.	fame	_____	_____
4.	soft	_____	_____
5.	down	_____	_____
6.	light	_____	_____
7.	east	_____	_____
8.	honor	_____	_____
9.	thank	_____	_____
10.	rest	_____	_____
11.	child	_____	_____
12.	remark	_____	_____
13.	violin	_____	_____
14.	courage	_____	_____
15.	worth	_____	_____

Name _____   Date _____

Contractions

> - A **contraction** is a word formed by joining two other words.
> - An **apostrophe** shows where a letter or letters have been omitted.
>   EXAMPLE: had not = hadn't
> - <u>Won't</u> is an exception.
>   EXAMPLE: will not = won't

A. Write the contraction for each pair of words.

1. did not _____
2. was not _____
3. we are _____
4. is not _____
5. who is _____
6. had not _____
7. I will _____
8. I am _____
9. it is _____
10. do not _____

11. they have _____
12. would not _____
13. will not _____
14. does not _____
15. were not _____
16. there is _____
17. could not _____
18. I have _____
19. she will _____
20. they are _____

B. Underline each contraction. Write the words that make up the contraction on the lines.

1. They're dusting the piano very carefully before they inspect it. _____

2. They'll want to look closely, in case there are any scratches. _____

3. If it's in good condition, Mary will buy it. _____

4. Mary's an excellent piano player. _____

5. Her friends think she'll earn a college scholarship with her talent. _____

6. Tom doesn't play the piano, but he's a great cook. _____ _____

7. He'd like to be a professional chef. _____

8. His friends would've liked for him to go to college. _____

9. But they aren't concerned as long as Tom's happy. _____ _____

10. Tom and Mary think they've got very supportive friends. _____

Name _____   Date _____

Compound Words

> - A **compound word** is a word that is made up of two or more words. The meaning of many compound words is related to the meaning of each individual word.
>   EXAMPLE: blue + berry = blueberry, meaning "a type of berry that is blue in color"
> - Compound words may be written as one word, as hyphenated words, or as two separate words. Always check a dictionary.

A. Combine the words in the list to make compound words. You may use words more than once.

air	knob	door	port	paper	condition	black	berry
sand	line	stand	under	way	ground	bird	sea

1. _____   7. _____

2. _____   8. _____

3. _____   9. _____

4. _____   10. _____

5. _____   11. _____

6. _____   12. _____

B. Answer the following questions.

1. Whirl means "to move in circles." What is a whirlpool?

   _____

2. Since quick means "moves rapidly," what is quicksand?

   _____

3. Rattle means "to make sharp, short sounds quickly." What is a rattlesnake?

   _____

4. A ring is "a small, circular band." What is an earring?

   _____

5. Pool can mean "a group of people who do something together." What is a car pool?

   _____

6. A lace can be "a string or cord that is used to hold something together." What is a shoelace?

   _____

Connotation/Denotation

- The **denotation** of a word is its exact meaning as stated in a dictionary.
  EXAMPLE: The denotation of stingy is "ungenerous" or "miserly."
- The **connotation** of a word is an added meaning that suggests something positive or negative.
  EXAMPLES: **Negative:** Stingy suggests "ungenerous." Stingy has a negative connotation.
  Positive: Economical suggests "efficient" and "careful." Economical has a positive connotation.
- Some words are neutral. They do not suggest either good or bad feelings.
  EXAMPLES: garage, kitchen, roof

A. Write (–) if the underlined word has a negative connotation. Write (+) if it has a positive connotation. Write (N) if the word is neutral.

_____ 1. This is my house.

_____ 2. This is my home.

_____ 3. Darren's friends discussed his problem.

_____ 4. Darren's friends gossiped about his problem.

_____ 5. Our dog is sick.

_____ 6. Our dog is diseased.

_____ 7. The play was enjoyable.

_____ 8. The play was fantastic.

_____ 9. Julie is boring.

_____ 10. Julie is quiet.

B. Fill each blank with the word that suggests the connotation given.

1. Our experience of the storm was _____. (negative)

2. Our experience of the storm was _____. (positive)

3. Our experience of the storm was _____. (neutral)

unpleasant
exciting
horrible

4. Monica is _____. (neutral)

5. Monica is _____. (positive)

6. Monica is _____. (negative)

old
over-the-hill
mature

Idioms

> ■ An **idiom** is an expression that has a meaning different from the usual meanings of the individual words within it.
> EXAMPLE: <u>Lit a fire under me</u> means "got me going," not "burned me."

A. Underline the idiom in each sentence. Then write what the idiom means.

1. Jack and Ellen knew they were in hot water when their car died.

   _____

2. They were miles from any town, and Ellen was beside herself.

   _____

3. Jack said they should put their heads together and find a solution.

   _____

4. Ellen told Jack that if he had any ideas, she was all ears.

   _____

5. Jack told her it was too soon to throw in the towel.

   _____

B. Underline each idiom. Then write one definition that tells the exact meaning of the phrase and another definition that tells what the phrase means in the sentence.

1. When I finish the test, I'm going to hit the road.

   a. ___Pound on the street_____

   b. ___Leave_____

2. I had to eat crow when I found out I was wrong about the test date.

   a. _____

   b. _____

3. With final exams coming, I'll have to burn the midnight oil.

   a. _____

   b. _____

4. I thought I was so smart, but that test really cut me down to size.

   a. _____

   b. _____

Unit 1 Test

Choose whether the underlined words in each sentence are synonyms, antonyms, homonyms, or homographs.

1. Her office is up the stairs and down the hall on the left.

   A ○ synonym   **B** ○ antonym   **C** ○ homonym   **D** ○ homograph

2. Let's sit here so that we can hear the music well.

   A ○ synonym   **B** ○ antonym   **C** ○ homonym   **D** ○ homograph

3. As I looked over my shoulder, I saw lightning strike a tree.

   A ○ synonym   **B** ○ antonym   **C** ○ homonym   **D** ○ homograph

4. We saw a fan using a fan to stay cool at the baseball game.

   A ○ synonym   **B** ○ antonym   **C** ○ homonym   **D** ○ homograph

5. He uses his left hand to throw and his right hand to write.

   A ○ synonym   **B** ○ antonym   **C** ○ homonym   **D** ○ homograph

6. Her error was more than a simple mistake.

   A ○ synonym   **B** ○ antonym   **C** ○ homonym   **D** ○ homograph

7. Nobody believed the man's account of where he got the money in his account.

   A ○ synonym   **B** ○ antonym   **C** ○ homonym   **D** ○ homograph

8. Erica found the book her sister thought she had lost.

   A ○ synonym   **B** ○ antonym   **C** ○ homonym   **D** ○ homograph

Add a prefix or suffix to the underlined word to make a new word that makes sense in the sentence.

9. Hard work and luck can make you fame.

   A ○ -ist   **C** ○ -ous

   B ○ -ward   **D** ○ re-

10. Only criminals port illegal drugs.

    A ○ mis-   **C** ○ -able

    B ○ trans-   **D** ○ re-

11. People who think of others are self.

    A ○ -less   **C** ○ -ous

    B ○ -ish   **D** ○ un-

12. Do you see any problems with this?

    A ○ pre-   **C** ○ with-

    B ○ -able   **D** ○ fore-

13. You will need depend transportation.

    A ○ pre-   **C** ○ -ous

    B ○ -able   **D** ○ re-

14. I sometimes place my glasses.

    A ○ mis-   **C** ○ -ly

    B ○ im-   **D** ○ -ful

15. That is a profit organization.

    A ○ un-   **C** ○ non-

    B ○ -ly   **D** ○ -ous

16. The road was rock.

    A ○ -ist   **C** ○ non-

    B ○ -ward   **D** ○ -y

Choose the correct contraction for each pair of underlined words.

17. there is

A ○ ther's   C ○ theres

B ○ there's   D ○ theres'

20. must not

A ○ musn't   C ○ mustnt

B ○ must'nt   D ○ mustn't

18. who have

A ○ who've   C ○ whov'e

B ○ wh've   D ○ who'v

21. will not

A ○ willn't   C ○ wo'nt

B ○ won't   D ○ wont

19. they will

A ○ the'yll   C ○ they'll

B ○ the'll   D ○ theyll'

22. she would

A ○ shed   C ○ shel'd

B ○ she'ld   D ○ she'd

Choose whether each underlined word has a positive connotation (+), a negative connotation (–), or is neutral (N).

23. We found a scrawny dog.   A ○ (+)   B ○ (–)   C ○ (N)

24. This book is interesting.   A ○ (+)   B ○ (–)   C ○ (N)

25. There's a small animal.   A ○ (+)   B ○ (–)   C ○ (N)

26. It was a foolish choice.   A ○ (+)   B ○ (–)   C ○ (N)

27. He has a unique idea.   A ○ (+)   B ○ (–)   C ○ (N)

28. The man had a big smile.   A ○ (+)   B ○ (–)   C ○ (N)

29. She is not a lazy person.   A ○ (+)   B ○ (–)   C ○ (N)

30. Please write to me sometime.   A ○ (+)   B ○ (–)   C ○ (N)

Choose the meaning of the underlined idiom.

31. keep your chin up

A ○ do less than you should   C ○ accept defeat

B ○ look straight ahead   D ○ have hope

34. beside yourself

A ○ unbelievably happy   C ○ spend money carefully

B ○ very upset   D ○ standing close

32. run across

A ○ play music   C ○ in a risky situation

B ○ meet by chance D ○ run over

35. all ears

A ○ listen carefully   C ○ have large ears

B ○ meet by chance   D ○ think about

33. turn over a new leaf

A ○ change your ways   C ○ rake leaves

B ○ admit   D ○ be in trouble

36. talk turkey

A ○ discuss a special meal   C ○ come through

B ○ stand up for   D ○ speak frankly

Name _____   Date _____

Recognizing Sentences

> ■ A **sentence** is a group of words that expresses a complete thought.
> EXAMPLE: We found a deserted cabin at the top of the hill.

■ **Some of the following groups of words are sentences, and some are not. Write S before each group that is a sentence. Punctuate each sentence with a period.**

_____ 1. Tomás did not go to the auto show____

_____ 2. By the side of the babbling brook____

_____ 3. I went to the new museum last week____

_____ 4. Mile after mile along the great highway____

_____ 5. Check all work carefully____

_____ 6. Down the narrow aisle of the church____

_____ 7. I have lost my hat____

_____ 8. On our way to work this morning____

_____ 9. Leontyne Price, a famous singer____

_____ 10. We saw Katherine and Sheryl yesterday____

_____ 11. The severe cold of last winter____

_____ 12. Once upon a time, long, long ago____

_____ 13. There was a gorgeous sunset last night____

_____ 14. He ran home____

_____ 15. My brother and my sister____

_____ 16. Tom and Matt did a great job____

_____ 17. We saw a beaver in the deep ravine____

_____ 18. The cat in our neighbor's yard____

_____ 19. Every year at the state fair____

_____ 20. As we came to the sharp curve in the road____

_____ 21. Just before we were ready____

_____ 22. I heard that you and Lorenzo have a new paper route____

_____ 23. Longfellow is called the children's poet____

_____ 24. Into the parking garage____

_____ 25. We washed and waxed the truck____

_____ 26. Through the door and up the stairs____

_____ 27. As quickly as possible____

_____ 28. We saw the new killer whale at the zoo____

_____ 29. John parked the car on the street____

_____ 30. We had ice cream and fruit for dessert____

Types of Sentences

- A **declarative sentence** makes a statement. It is followed by a period (.).   EXAMPLE: Alicia is my cousin.
- An **interrogative sentence** asks a question. It is followed by a question mark (?).   EXAMPLE: Where are you going?
- An **imperative sentence** expresses a command or request. It is followed by a period (.).   EXAMPLE: Close the door.
- An **exclamatory sentence** expresses strong emotion. It can also express a command or request that is made with great excitement. It is followed by an exclamation mark (!).   EXAMPLES: How you frightened me! Look at that accident!

A. Write **D** for declarative, **IN** for interrogative, **IM** for imperative, or **E** for exclamatory before each sentence. Put the correct punctuation at the end of each sentence.

_____ **1.** Everyone will be here by nine o'clock____

_____ **2.** Train your mind to do its work efficiently____

_____ **3.** How does a canal lock work____

_____ **4.** Prepare each day's assignment on time____

_____ **5.** Are we going to the game now____

_____ **6.** Who brought these delicious peaches____

_____ **7.** Our guests have arrived____

_____ **8.** What is meant by rotation of crops____

_____ **9.** Please bring a glass of water____

_____ **10.** Stop that noise____

_____ **11.** Always stand erect____

_____ **12.** Who arranged these flowers____

_____ **13.** Anna, what do you have in that box____

_____ **14.** The Vikings were famous sailors____

_____ **15.** Have you solved all the problems in our lesson____

_____ **16.** Jack, hand me that wrench____

_____ **17.** What is the capital of California____

_____ **18.** Cultivate a pleasant manner____

_____ **19.** How is a pizza made____

_____ **20.** Block that kick____

_____ **21.** A nation is measured by the character of its people____

_____ **22.** Are you an early riser____

_____ **23.** Practice good table manners____

_____ **24.** What a wonderful time we've had____

_____ **25.** How did you get here so early____

_____ **26.** Look out for those cars____

_____ **27.** Take good care of my dog____

_____ **28.** There are many cotton mills in our state____

_____ **29.** Name the capital of Nevada____

_____ **30.** Hurrah, the game is over____

_____ **31.** Draw a map of South America____

_____ **32.** Geysers were first discovered in Iceland____

_____ **33.** Have you ever been on a roller coaster____

_____ **34.** Sweep the front walk____

_____ **35.** Do not measure people by what they have____

_____ **36.** A great nation is made only by worthy citizens____

_____ **37.** Anna Moffo has sung with many of the major opera companies____

_____ **38.** What is the longest river in the country____

_____ **39.** Oh, you have a new car____

_____ **40.** Andrea, why weren't you at the meeting____

_____ **41.** The organization will elect officers tomorrow____

_____ **42.** Chris, I have a long piece of twine____

_____ **43.** Paul, jump quickly____

B. **Only one group of words in each pair below is a sentence. Circle the sentence, and tell what kind it is. Write D for declarative, IN for interrogative, IM for imperative, or E for exclamatory.**

_____ **1.** When will the train arrive? Two hours late.

_____ **2.** It is delayed by bad weather. Not here yet.

_____ **3.** From California. Juan and Shelly are on it.

_____ **4.** I haven't seen them in two years! Am waiting patiently.

_____ **5.** Enjoy traveling. They will stay with us for two weeks.

_____ **6.** We have many things planned for them. A good visit.

_____ **7.** Sleep in the guest room. To our city's new zoo?

_____ **8.** Juan used to work at a zoo. Many animals.

_____ **9.** Go in the reptile house. Took care of the elephants.

_____ **10.** Each elephant had a name. Wally, Sandra, and Joe.

_____ **11.** The elephants liked to train with Juan. Good job.

_____ **12.** Sandra, the elephant, had a baby. In the zoo.

_____ **13.** Male elephant. What did the zoo officials name the baby?

_____ **14.** People in the zoo. They surprised Juan!

_____ **15.** He never had an elephant named for him before! Seal exhibit.

Complete Subjects and Predicates

- Every sentence has two main parts, a **complete subject** and a **complete predicate.**
- The complete subject includes all the words that tell who or what the sentence is about.   EXAMPLE: **All chickadees**/hunt insect eggs.
- The complete predicate includes all the words that state the action or condition of the subject.   EXAMPLE: All chickadees/**hunt insect eggs.**

A. Draw a line between the complete subject and the complete predicate in each sentence below.

1. Amy/built a bird feeder for the backyard.
2. This cleaner will remove paint.
3. Many beautiful waltzes were composed by Johann Strauss.
4. Queen Victoria ruled England for many years.
5. Eighty people are waiting in line for tickets.
6. Mario's last visit was during the summer.
7. The rocket was soon in orbit.
8. Our last meeting was held in my living room.
9. The farmers are harvesting their wheat.
10. Our new house has six rooms.
11. The heart pumps blood throughout the body.
12. This computer will help you work faster.
13. My friend has moved to Santa Fe, New Mexico.
14. A deep silence fell upon the crowd.
15. The police officers were stopping the speeding motorists.
16. The French chef prepared excellent food.
17. My father is a mechanic.
18. José Salazar is running for the city council.
19. Lightning struck a tree in our yard.
20. Magazines about bicycling are becoming increasingly popular.
21. They answered every question honestly during the interview.
22. The gray twilight came before the program ended.
23. Steve has a way with words.
24. That section of the country has many pine forests.
25. We will have a party for Teresa on Friday.
26. Butterflies flew around the flowers.
27. The heavy bus was stuck in the mud.

Name _____ Date _____

B. Write a sentence by adding a complete predicate to each complete subject.

1. All of the students _____

2. Elephants _____

3. The top of the mountain _____

4. The television programs tonight _____

5. I _____

6. Each of the girls _____

7. My father's truck _____

8. The dam across the river _____

9. Our new station wagon _____

10. You _____

11. The books in our bookcase _____

12. The mountains _____

13. Today's paper _____

14. The magazine staff _____

C. Write a sentence by adding a complete subject to each complete predicate.

1. _____ is the largest city in Mexico.

2. _____ came to our program.

3. _____ is a valuable mineral.

4. _____ grow beside the road.

5. _____ traveled day and night.

6. _____ was a great inventor.

7. _____ wrote the letter of complaint.

8. _____ met us at the airport.

9. _____ made ice cream for the picnic.

10. _____ made a nest in our tree.

11. _____ lives near the shopping center.

12. _____ have a meeting on Saturday.

Simple Subjects and Predicates

> ■ The **simple subject** of a sentence is the main word in the complete subject. The simple subject is a noun or a pronoun. Sometimes the simple subject is also the complete subject. EXAMPLES: Our **car**/swayed in the strong wind. **Cars**/sway in the strong wind.

A. Draw a line between the complete subject and the complete predicate in each sentence below. Then underline the simple subject.

1. The plants sprouted quickly after the first rain.

2. The television program was very informative.

3. I used a word processor to write the paper.

4. My friend's truck is parked in the driveway.

5. The beavers created a dam in the river.

6. The books lined the shelves like toy soldiers.

7. Hail pounded against the storm door.

8. I bought a new mountain bike.

9. My favorite subject is history.

10. The colorful bird sang a beautiful melody.

11. The tree trunk was about five feet in diameter.

12. The sidewalk had cracks in the pavement.

> ■ The **simple predicate** of a sentence is a verb within the complete predicate. The simple predicate may be made up of one word or more than one word. EXAMPLES: Our car/**swayed.** The wind/**was blowing** hard.

B. In each sentence below, draw a line between the complete subject and the complete predicate. Underline the simple predicate twice.

1. A rare Chinese vase was on display.

2. Many of the children had played.

3. All of the group went on a hike.

4. He drove the bus slowly over the slippery pavement.

5. A large number of water-skiers were on the lake last Saturday.

6. Birds have good eyesight.

7. Who discovered the Pacific Ocean?

8. I am reading the assignment now.

9. The glare of the headlights blinded us.

10. The problem on the next page is harder.

Position of Subjects

- When the subject of a sentence comes before the verb, the sentence is in **natural order.**   EXAMPLE: <u>Maria</u> <u>went</u> home.
- When the verb or part of the verb comes before the subject, the sentence is in **inverted order.**   EXAMPLES: On the branch <u>were</u> two <u>birds</u>.
    There <u>are</u> four <u>children</u> in my family. Here <u>is</u> my <u>friend</u>.
- Many questions are in inverted order.   EXAMPLE: Where <u>is</u> <u>Jim</u>?
- Sometimes the subject of a sentence is not expressed, as in a command or request. The understood subject is <u>you</u>.   EXAMPLES: <u>Bring</u> the sandwiches. (<u>You</u>) <u>bring</u> the sandwiches.

■ **Rewrite each inverted sentence in natural order. Rewrite commands or requests by including <u>you</u> as the subject. Then underline each simple subject once and each simple predicate twice in each sentence you write.**

1. Where was the sunken treasure ship?

   The sunken treasure <u>ship</u> <u>was</u> where?
   _____

2. Beyond the bridge were several sailboats.

   _____

3. There is no one in that room.

   _____

4. From the gymnasium came the shouts of the victorious team.

   _____

5. Beside the walk grew beautiful flowers.

   _____

6. When is the surprise party?

   _____

7. Bring your sales report to the meeting.

   _____

8. There were only three floats in the parade.

   _____

9. From the yard came the bark of a dog.

   _____

10. Place the forks to the left of the plate.

    _____

Compound Subjects

> ■ A **compound subject** is made up of two or more simple subjects.
> EXAMPLE: **Henri** and **Tanya** / are tall people.

A. Draw a line between the complete subject and the complete predicate in each sentence. Write SS for a simple subject. Write CS for a compound subject.

_CS_   **1.** Arturo and I/often work late on Friday.

_____   **2.** Sandy left the person near the crowded exit.

_____   **3.** She and I will mail the packages to San Francisco, California, today.

_____   **4.** Shanghai and New Delhi are two cities visited by the group.

_____   **5.** The fire spread rapidly to other buildings in the neighborhood.

_____   **6.** Luis and Lenora helped their parents with the chores.

_____   **7.** Swimming, jogging, and hiking were our favorite sports.

_____   **8.** Melbourne and Sydney are important Australian cities.

_____   **9.** Eric and I had an interesting experience Saturday.

_____   **10.** The Red Sea and the Mediterranean Sea are connected by the Suez Canal.

_____   **11.** The Republicans and the Democrats made many speeches before the election.

_____   **12.** The people waved to us from the top of the cliff.

_____   **13.** Liz and Jim crated the freshly-picked apples.

_____   **14.** Clean clothes and a neat appearance are important in an interview.

_____   **15.** The kitten and the old dog are good friends.

_____   **16.** David and Paul are on their way to the swimming pool.

_____   **17.** Tom combed his dog's shiny black coat.

_____   **18.** Redbud and dogwood trees bloom in the spring.

_____   **19.** I hummed a cheerful tune on the way to the meeting.

_____   **20.** Buffalo, deer, and antelope once roamed the plains of North America.

_____   **21.** Gina and Hiroshi raked the leaves.

_____   **22.** Brasília and São Paulo are two cities in Brazil.

_____   **23.** Hang gliding is a popular sport in Hawaii.

_____   **24.** Our class went on a field trip to the aquarium.

_____   **25.** The doctor asked him to get a blood test.

B. Write two sentences containing compound subjects.

1. _____

2. _____

Name _____ Date _____

Compound Predicates

■ A **compound predicate** is made up of two or more simple predicates.
EXAMPLE: Joseph / **dances** and **sings**.

A. Draw a line between the complete subject and the complete predicate in each sentence. Write SP for each simple predicate. Write CP for each compound predicate.

_CP_   **1.** Edward / grinned and nodded.

_____   **2.** Plants need air to live.

_____   **3.** Old silver tea kettles were among their possessions.

_____   **4.** My sister buys and sells real estate.

_____   **5.** Snow covered every highway in the area.

_____   **6.** Mr. Sanders designs and makes odd pieces of furniture.

_____   **7.** Popcorn is one of my favorite snack foods.

_____   **8.** Soccer is one of my favorite sports.

_____   **9.** The ducks quickly crossed the road and found the ducklings.

_____   **10.** They came early and stayed late.

_____   **11.** Crystal participated in the Special Olympics this year.

_____   **12.** José raked and sacked the leaves.

_____   **13.** Perry built the fire and cooked supper.

_____   **14.** We collected old newspapers for the recycling center.

_____   **15.** Doug arrived in Toronto, Ontario, during the afternoon.

_____   **16.** Tony's parents are visiting in Oregon and Washington.

_____   **17.** The Garzas live in that apartment building on Oak Street.

_____   **18.** The shingles were picked up and delivered today.

_____   **19.** The audience talked and laughed before the performance.

_____   **20.** Automobiles crowd and jam that highway early in the morning.

_____   **21.** The apples are rotting in the boxes.

_____   **22.** The leader of the group grumbled and scolded.

_____   **23.** She worked hard and waited patiently.

_____   **24.** Nelson Mandela is a great civil rights activist.

_____   **25.** The supervisor has completed the work for the week.

B. Write two sentences containing compound predicates.

1. _____

2. _____

Combining Sentences

> - Two sentences in which the subjects are different and the predicates are the same can be combined into one sentence. The two subjects are joined by <u>and</u>.   EXAMPLE: **Hurricanes** are storms. **Tornadoes** are storms. **Hurricanes and tornadoes** are storms.
> - Two sentences in which the subjects are the same and the predicates are different can be combined into one sentence. The two predicates may be joined by <u>or</u>, <u>and</u>, or <u>but</u>.   EXAMPLE: Hurricanes **begin over tropical oceans.** Hurricanes **move inland.** Hurricanes **begin over tropical oceans and move inland.**

■ **Combine each pair of sentences below. Underline the compound subject or the compound predicate in each sentence that you write.**

1. Lightning is part of a thunderstorm. Thunder is part of a thunderstorm.

   _____

2. Thunderstorms usually happen in the spring. Thunderstorms bring heavy rains.

   _____

3. Depending on how close or far away it is, thunder sounds like a sharp crack.
   Depending on how close or far away it is, thunder rumbles.

   _____

   _____

4. Lightning is very exciting to watch. Lightning can be very dangerous.

   _____

5. Lightning causes many fires. Lightning harms many people.

   _____

6. An open field is an unsafe place to be during a thunderstorm.
   A golf course is an unsafe place to be during a thunderstorm.

   _____

   _____

7. Benjamin Franklin wanted to protect people from lightning.
   Benjamin Franklin invented the lightning rod.

   _____

   _____

8. A lightning rod is a metal rod placed on the top of a building.
   A lightning rod is connected to the ground by a cable.

   _____

   _____

Direct Objects

> ■ The **direct object** tells who or what receives the action of the verb. The direct object is a noun or pronoun that follows an action verb.
>
> EXAMPLE: You told the **truth**.
> (DO above **truth**)

■ **Underline the verb in each sentence. Then write DO above each direct object.**

1. Elephants <u>can carry</u> logs (DO) with their trunks.

2. Who made this magazine rack?

3. Do you always plan a daily schedule?

4. They easily won the game.

5. Martin baked an apple pie for dinner.

6. Who tuned your piano?

7. I take guitar lessons once a week.

8. Who composed this melody?

9. I especially enjoy mystery stories.

10. The astronauts orbited the earth many times.

11. I bought this coat in New York.

12. Did he find his glasses?

13. Anne drove the truck to the hardware store.

14. The boy shrugged his shoulders.

15. We have finished our work today.

16. We drink milk with breakfast.

17. She can solve any problem quickly.

18. Who made our first flag?

19. You will learn something from this lesson.

20. Every person needs friends.

21. I have found a dime.

22. Yuko ate an apple for a snack.

Indirect Objects

> ■ The **indirect object** is the noun or pronoun that tells to whom or for whom an action is done. In order to have an indirect object, a sentence must have a direct object.
> ■ The indirect object is usually placed between the action verb and the direct object.
> EXAMPLE: Who sold **you** that fantastic **bike?**
> $\qquad\qquad\qquad\quad$ IO $\qquad\qquad\qquad$ DO

■ **Underline the verb in each sentence. Then write <u>DO</u> above the direct object and <u>IO</u> above the indirect object.**

1. Certain marine plants <u>give</u> the Red Sea its color.
   $\qquad\qquad\qquad\qquad\qquad$ IO $\qquad$ DO

2. I gave the cashier a check for twenty dollars.

3. The magician showed the audience a few of her tricks.

4. The coach taught them the rules of the game.

5. Roberto brought us some foreign coins.

6. This interesting book will give every reader pleasure.

7. Have you written your brother a letter?

8. They made us some sandwiches to take on our hike.

9. The astronaut gave Mission Control the data.

10. I bought my friend an etching at the art exhibit.

11. James, did you sell Mike your car?

12. We have given the dog a thorough scrubbing.

13. Give the usher your ticket.

14. Carl brought my brother a gold ring from Mexico.

15. Hand me a pencil, please.

16. The conductor gave the orchestra a short break.

17. Show me the picture of your boat.

18. I have given you my money.

19. Give Lee this message.

20. The club gave the town a new statue.

Independent and Subordinate Clauses

> - A **clause** is a group of words that contains a subject and a predicate. There are two kinds of clauses: **independent clauses** and **subordinate clauses.**
> - An **independent clause** can stand alone as a sentence because it expresses a complete thought.
>   EXAMPLE: **The students came in** when the bell rang. **The students came in.**

A. Underline the independent clause in each sentence below.

1. Frank will be busy because he is studying.

2. I have only one hour that I can spare.

3. The project must be finished when I get back.

4. Gloria volunteered to do the typing that needs to be done.

5. The work is going too slowly for us to finish on time.

6. Before Nathan started to help, I didn't think we could finish.

7. What else should we do before we relax?

8. Since you forgot to give this page to Gloria, you can type it.

9. After she had finished typing, we completed the project.

10. We actually got it finished before the deadline.

> - A **subordinate clause** has a subject and predicate but cannot stand alone as a sentence because it does not express a complete thought. A subordinate clause must be combined with an independent clause to make a sentence.
>   EXAMPLE: The stamp **that I bought** was already in my collection.

B. Underline the subordinate clause in each sentence below.

1. The people who went shopping found a great sale.

2. Tony's bike, which is a mountain bike, came from that store.

3. Juana was sad when the sale was over.

4. Marianne was excited because she wanted some new things.

5. Thomas didn't find anything since he went late.

6. The mall where we went shopping was new.

7. The people who own the stores are proud of the beautiful setting.

8. The mall, which is miles away, is serviced by the city bus.

9. We ran as fast as we could because the bus was coming.

10. We were panting because we had run fast.

Adjective Clauses

■ An **adjective clause** is a subordinate clause that modifies a noun or a pronoun. It answers the adjective question <u>Which one?</u> or <u>What kind?</u> It usually modifies the word directly preceding it. Most adjective clauses begin with a **relative pronoun**. A relative pronoun relates an adjective clause to the noun or pronoun that the clause modifies. <u>Who</u>, <u>whose</u>, <u>which</u>, and <u>that</u> are relative pronouns.

EXAMPLE: The <u>coat</u> **that I bought** was on sale.
noun adjective clause

A. Underline the adjective clause in each sentence below.

1. A compass has a needle that always points northward.

2. A seismograph is an instrument that measures earthquake tremors.

3. People who work in science laboratories today have a broad field of study.

4. This will be the first time that she has played in that position.

5. Jay is the person whose wrist was broken.

6. The fish that I caught was large.

7. A sentence that contains a subordinate clause is a complex sentence.

8. Here is the photograph that I promised to show you.

9. The book that I read was very humorous.

B. Add an adjective clause to each independent clause below.

1. A microscope is an instrument   (that) _____

_____

2. Amelia Earhart was a pilot   (who) _____

_____

3. We have football players   (who) _____

_____

4. They built a helicopter   (which) _____

_____

5. Bunny is a dog   (that) _____

_____

6. A telescope is an instrument   (that) _____

_____

Adverb Clauses

> ■ An **adverb clause** is a subordinate clause that modifies a verb, an adjective, or another adverb. It answers the adverb question <u>How?</u> <u>Under what condition?</u> or <u>Why?</u> Words that introduce adverb clauses are called **subordinating conjunctions.** The many subordinating conjunctions include such words as <u>when</u>, <u>after</u>, <u>before</u>, <u>since</u>, <u>although</u>, and <u>because</u>.   EXAMPLE: I finished **before the bell rang.**
>   adverb clause

A. Underline the adverb clause in each sentence below.

1. We had agreed to go hiking when the cloudy skies cleared.

2. Although the weather was mild and sunny, we took along our jackets.

3. Clouds began to move in once again after we arrived at the park.

4. We felt comfortable about the weather because we were prepared.

5. Since we had our jackets, we didn't get too cold.

6. Although the clouds remained, it never rained.

7. It was exhilarating to see the view when we got to the top of the hill.

8. After enjoying the beauty and the quiet for a while, we hiked back down.

9. We decided to drive home the long way since it was still early.

10. We had a wonderful day because we were so relaxed and happy.

B. Add an adverb clause to each independent clause below.

1. We ate breakfast   (before) _____

_____

2. Jay and I carried umbrellas   (since) _____

_____

3. We took the bus to the museum   (because) _____

_____

4. People in line waited   (when) _____

_____

5. We saw the exhibit   (after) _____

_____

6. Joel and I baked cookies   (when) _____

_____

Simple and Compound Sentences

- A **simple sentence** contains only one independent clause. The subject, the predicate, or both may be compound.
  EXAMPLES: The courthouse/is the oldest building in town. Gale and Louise/are making costumes and dressing up.
- A **compound sentence** consists of two or more independent clauses. Each independent clause in a compound sentence can stand alone as a separate sentence. The independent clauses are usually joined by <u>and</u>, <u>but</u>, <u>so</u>, <u>or</u>, <u>for</u>, or <u>yet</u> and a comma.
  EXAMPLE: Jack brought the chairs, but Mary forgot the extra table.
- Sometimes a **semicolon (;)** is used to join two independent clauses in a compound sentence.
  EXAMPLE: The music started; the dance had begun.

A. Write <u>S</u> before each simple sentence, and write <u>CS</u> before each compound sentence.

_____ **1.** We can wait for James, or we can go on ahead.

_____ **2.** The carnival will start today in the empty lot.

_____ **3.** Jack and Manuel are going to meet us there at six o'clock.

_____ **4.** I really want to go to the carnival, yet I am not sure about going tonight.

_____ **5.** I didn't mean to hurt Carl's feelings by not going.

_____ **6.** You wait for the package, and I'll meet you at the carnival.

_____ **7.** I can't skip my homework to go, but maybe I'll finish it this afternoon.

_____ **8.** Jan and Alicia are both working at the carnival this year.

B. Put brackets ([ ]) around the independent clauses in each compound sentence. Then underline the word or punctuation used to join the clauses.

1. You must observe all the rules, or you must withdraw from the race.

2. I did well on the test, and Maria did well, too.

3. Shall I carry this box, or do you want to leave it here?

4. We must closely guard our freedom, or an enemy will take it from us.

5. He threw a beautiful pass, but no one caught it.

6. The doctor treated the cut, but he did not have to make any stitches.

7. I like to spend weekends at home, but the others prefer to travel.

8. The year is almost over, and everyone is thinking of the new year.

9. The family faced every hardship, yet they were thankful for what they had.

10. Move the box over here; I'll unpack it.

11. Connie likes football; James prefers hockey.

12. I drive safely, but I always make everyone fasten seat belts.

13. Please get the telephone number, and I'll call after work.

Complex Sentences

> ■ A **complex sentence** contains one independent clause and one or more subordinate clauses.
>
> EXAMPLE: The person **who helps me carry these** gets some dessert.
> subordinate clause

A. Put brackets around the subordinate clause, and underline the independent clause in each complex sentence below.

1. The shadows [that had fallen between the trees] were a deep purple.

2. The soldiers waded across the stream where the water was shallow.

3. They waited for me until the last bus came.

4. The fans of that team were sad when the team lost the game.

5. When George was here, he was charmed by the beauty of the hills.

6. Sophia will call for you when she is ready.

7. Some spiders that are found in Sumatra have legs seventeen inches long.

8. Those who are going will arrive on time.

9. Do not throw the bat after you've hit the ball.

10. Tell us about the trip that you made a year ago.

B. Add a subordinate clause that begins with the word in parentheses to make a complex sentence.

1. I try not to drive   (where) _____

_____

2. The electric light is an important invention   (that) _____

_____

3. The telephone stopped ringing   (before) _____

_____

4. He is the man   (who) _____

_____

5. This is the book   (that) _____

_____

6. Turn to the left   (when) _____

_____

Correcting Run–on Sentences

- Two or more independent clauses that are run together without the correct punctuation are called a **run-on sentence.**
  - EXAMPLE: The music was deafening I turned down the volume.
- One way to correct a run-on sentence is to separate it into two sentences.
  - EXAMPLE: The music was deafening. I turned down the volume.
- Another way to correct a run-on sentence is to make it into a compound sentence.
  - EXAMPLE: The music was deafening, so I turned down the volume.
- Another way to correct a run-on sentence is to use a semicolon.
  - EXAMPLE: The music was deafening; I turned down the volume.

■ **Correct each run-on sentence below by writing it as two sentences or as a compound sentence.**

1. The city council held a meeting a meeting is held every month.

   _____

   _____

2. The council members are elected by the voters there are two thousand voters in the city.

   _____

   _____

3. There is one council member from each suburb, the president is elected by the council members.

   _____

   _____

4. Those who run for office must give speeches, the speeches should be short.

   _____

   _____

5. The council decides on many activities every activity is voted on.

   _____

   _____

6. Money is needed for many of the special activities, the council also plans fund-raisers in the city.

   _____

   _____

7. The annual city picnic is sponsored by the city council the picnic is in May.

   _____

   _____

Expanding Sentences

> ■ Sentences can be **expanded** by adding details to make them clearer and more interesting.   EXAMPLE: The audience laughed. The **excited** audience **in the theater** laughed **loudly.**
>
> ■ Details added to sentences may answer these questions: When? Where? How? How often? To what degree? What kind? Which? How many?

A. Expand each sentence below by adding details to answer the questions shown in parentheses. Write the expanded sentence on the line.

1. The car stalled.   (What kind? Where?)

_____

2. Mary raised the hood.   (How? Which?)

_____

3. Smoke billowed from the engine.   (What kind? Where?)

_____

4. She called the service station.   (When? Which?)

_____

5. The phone rang.   (Which? How often?)

_____

B. Decide how each of the following sentences can be expanded. Write your expanded sentence on the line.

1. The runner crossed the finish line.

_____

2. The crowd cheered.

_____

3. The reporter interviewed her.

_____

4. She answered.

_____

5. Her coach ran up to her.

_____

6. She and her coach walked off the track.

_____

7. She was awarded the medal.

_____

Unit 2 Test

Choose (A) if the sentence is declarative, (B) if it is interrogative, (C) if it is imperative, or (D) if it is exclamatory.

1. Please answer the front door.   **A** ○   **B** ○   **C** ○   **D** ○

2. Who's at the door?   **A** ○   **B** ○   **C** ○   **D** ○

3. It's your friend Jesse.   **A** ○   **B** ○   **C** ○   **D** ○

4. I can't believe it!   **A** ○   **B** ○   **C** ○   **D** ○

Choose the correct end punctuation for each sentence.

5. You scared me to death   **A** ○ .   **B** ○ ?   **C** ○ !

6. Why are you doing that   **A** ○ .   **B** ○ ?   **C** ○ !

7. Please get some more ice   **A** ○ .   **B** ○ ?   **C** ○ !

8. I think it's going to rain   **A** ○ .   **B** ○ ?   **C** ○ !

Choose the sentences that have a line drawn between the complete subject and the complete predicate.

9. **A** ○ Joanne writes / me every month.

   B ○ The newspaper told all / about the council meeting.

   C ○ Dana's cousin and his friend / are visiting for the week.

   D ○ It snowed / for the first time all winter.

10. **A** ○ The longest day / of the year is in June.

    B ○ Most of the people stood / in line for hours.

    C ○ All of the guests / enjoyed the party.

    D ○ Joe and Ming will be / leaving soon.

Choose the sentences in which the simple subject is underlined.

11. **A** ○ Their house is for sale.

    B ○ That is a great story.

    C ○ Our neighbors are very friendly.

    D ○ That store has many kinds of costumes.

12. **A** ○ The first thing to do is remove the cover.

    B ○ Her jacket was torn.

    C ○ The fresh bread smelled wonderful.

    D ○ The answer to the question was wrong.

Choose the sentence in which the simple predicate is underlined.

13. **A** ○ Carol had heard them at the concert.

    B ○ I can remember everyone who went.

    C ○ Paul has been practicing all morning.

    D ○ José brought some fresh vegetables.

Choose the sentence that is written in natural order.

14. **A** ○ Always this trip I will remember.

    B ○ Around the corner is the drugstore.

    C ○ The lights suddenly went out.

    D ○ Did you turn off the oven?

Choose the sentence that has a compound subject.

15. **A** ○ Juanita and Ted went to the movies.

B ○ Pearl, Lily's dog, came home muddy.

C ○ Exercise is good for your health.

D ○ The horse trotted and pranced.

Choose the sentence that has a compound predicate.

16. **A** ○ The clerk totaled the check.

B ○ Bob and Margie traveled to Europe.

C ○ The skater jumped and spun in the air.

D ○ The old oak tree split in half.

Identify each underlined word.

17. We brought them some souvenirs.

A ○ direct object

B ○ indirect object

Choose the type of clause underlined in each sentence.

19. We followed the crowd as it moved toward the exit.

A ○ independent

B ○ subordinate

18. Teresa sent me postcards from Italy.

A ○ direct object

B ○ indirect object

20. When the music stopped, everyone clapped.

A ○ independent

B ○ subordinate

Choose how the underlined subordinate clause is used in each sentence.

21. We went swimming when the weather improved.   **A** ○ adjective clause   **B** ○ adverb clause

22. The cabin that is next to ours is vacant.   **A** ○ adjective clause   **B** ○ adverb clause

Choose the correct description for each sentence.

23. Tony loves to go shopping.

A ○ simple   **C** ○ complex

B ○ compound   **D** ○ run-on

26. She prefers to buy only what she's looking for when she shops.

A ○ simple   **C** ○ complex

B ○ compound   **D** ○ run-on

24. He often asks Anika to go, sometimes she does.

A ○ simple   **C** ○ complex

B ○ compound   **D** ○ run-on

27. Tony, who loves browsing, would rather spend more time looking.

A ○ simple   **C** ○ complex

B ○ compound   **D** ○ run-on

25. They like to shop together, but Anika doesn't like to browse.

A ○ simple   **C** ○ complex

B ○ compound   **D** ○ run-on

28. They always agree on a plan, and then they both enjoy the outing.

A ○ simple   **C** ○ complex

B ○ compound   **D** ○ run-on

Name _____ Date _____

C. Write a proper noun suggested by each common noun.

1. continent _____

2. mountain _____

3. hotel _____

4. hero _____

5. inventor _____

6. building _____

7. day _____

8. physician _____

9. holiday _____

10. state _____

11. actor _____

12. magazine _____

13. month _____

14. lake _____

15. school _____

16. river _____

17. song _____

18. president _____

19. explorer _____

20. basketball team _____

D. Write a sentence in which you use a proper noun suggested to you by each phrase.

1. Your state or province _____

_____

2. Name of a foreign country _____

_____

3. Name of a singer _____

_____

4. Name of the make of an automobile _____

_____

5. Name of a store near your home _____

_____

6. Name of a television star _____

_____

7. Name of an ocean _____

_____

8. Name of the President of the United States _____

_____

Singular and Plural Nouns

The following chart shows how to change **singular nouns** into **plural nouns.**		
Noun	**Plural Form**	**Examples**
Most nouns	Add -s	ship, ships nose, noses
Nouns ending in a consonant and -y	Change the -y to -i, and add -es	sky, skies navy, navies
Nouns ending in -o	Add -s or -es	hero, heroes piano, pianos
Most nouns ending in -f or -fe	Change the -f or -fe to -ves	half, halves
Most nouns ending in -ch, -sh, -s, or -x	Add -es	bench, benches bush, bushes tax, taxes
Many two-word or three-word compound nouns	Add -s to the principle word	son-in-law, sons-in-law
Nouns with the same form in the singular and plural	No change	sheep

A. Fill in the blank with the plural form of the word in parentheses.

1. (brush)   These are plastic _____.

2. (lunch)   That cafe on the corner serves well-balanced _____.

3. (country)   What _____ belong to the United Nations?

4. (bench)   There are many iron _____ in the park.

5. (earring)   These _____ came from Italy.

6. (calf)   How many _____ are in that pen?

7. (piano)   There are three _____ in the warehouse.

8. (fox)   Did you see the _____ at the zoo?

9. (daisy)   We bought Susan a bunch of _____.

10. (potato)   Do you like baked _____?

11. (dish)   Please help wash the _____.

12. (store)   There are three _____ near my house.

Name _____ Date _____

B. Write the correct plural form for each singular noun.

1. booklet _____ 16. watch _____

2. tomato _____ 17. elf _____

3. truck _____ 18. desk _____

4. chef _____ 19. pan _____

5. branch _____ 20. sheep _____

6. toddler _____ 21. garden _____

7. penny _____ 22. pony _____

8. potato _____ 23. solo _____

9. piece _____ 24. tree _____

10. door _____ 25. light _____

11. island _____ 26. church _____

12. country _____ 27. city _____

13. house _____ 28. spoonful _____

14. garage _____ 29. vacation _____

15. fish _____ 30. home _____

C. Rewrite the sentences, changing each underlined singular noun to a plural noun.

1. Put the apple and orange in the box.

_____

2. Jan wrote five letter to her friend.

_____

3. Those building each have four elevator.

_____

4. Our family drove many mile to get to the lake.

_____

5. The top of those car were damaged in the storm.

_____

6. My aunt and uncle attended the family reunion.

_____

Possessive Nouns

> ■ A **possessive noun** shows possession of the noun that follows.
> ■ Form the possessive of most singular nouns by adding an apostrophe (') and -s.   EXAMPLES: a child's toy, my teacher's classroom
> ■ Form the possessive of plural nouns ending in -s by adding only an apostrophe.   EXAMPLES: our books' pages, those stores' windows
> ■ Form the possessive of plural nouns that do not end in -s by adding an apostrophe and -s.   EXAMPLES: some women's clothes, many men's shoes

A. Write the possessive form of each noun.

1. brother _____   **10.** man _____

2. boy _____   **11.** Dr. Kahn _____

3. Carol _____   **12.** soldier _____

4. children _____   **13.** pony _____

5. grandmother _____   **14.** friend _____

6. men _____   **15.** child _____

7. heroes _____   **16.** engineers _____

8. women _____   **17.** birds _____

9. ox _____   **18.** Jon _____

B. Write ten sentences using possessive nouns formed in Exercise A.

1. _____

2. _____

3. _____

4. _____

5. _____

6. _____

7. _____

8. _____

9. _____

10. _____

Name _____ Date _____

C. Complete each sentence with the possessive form of the word in parentheses.

1. (doctor) My _____ office is closed.

2. (senator) The _____ speech was astounding.

3. (sheep) What is the old saying about a wolf in _____ clothing?

4. (baby) Are the _____ hands cold?

5. (instructor) My _____ classroom is on this floor.

6. (collectors) Let's form a _____ club.

7. (spider) A _____ web has a complicated design.

8. (Mr. Takata) _____ store was damaged by the flood.

9. (Tim) _____ brother found this purse.

10. (Beth) _____ business is successful.

11. (Carl Sandburg) _____ poems are enjoyed by people of all ages.

12. (child) The _____ book is torn.

13. (women) That store sells _____ clothing.

14. (elephants) There were seats on the _____ backs.

15. (sister) My _____ room is at the front of the house.

16. (Brazil) What is the name of _____ largest river?

17. (friends) Those are my _____ homes.

18. (bird) That _____ nest is very close to the ground.

19. (children) The library has a table of _____ books.

20. (owl) I heard an _____ hoot during the night.

21. (brothers) Please get your _____ shirts from the dryer.

22. (student) The _____ pen ran out of ink.

23. (country) We sang our _____ national anthem.

24. (owner) The dog lay at its _____ feet.

25. (uncle) I visited my _____ laundry.

26. (Joan) _____ paintings sell well.

27. (men) The _____ jackets are brown.

Appositives

- An **appositive** is a noun that identifies or explains the noun or pronoun it follows.
  EXAMPLE: My dog, **Fido,** won a medal.
- An **appositive phrase** consists of an appositive and its modifiers.
  EXAMPLE: My book, **a novel about the Civil War,** is one of the best I've read.
- Use **commas** to set off an appositive or an appositive phrase that is not essential to the meaning of the sentence.
  EXAMPLE: John Gray, my uncle, owns that home.
- Don't use commas if the appositive is essential to the meaning of the sentence.
  EXAMPLES: My brother Kevin arrived late. My other brother Charlie arrived early.

A. Underline the appositive or appositive phrase, and circle the noun that it identifies.

1. Banff, the large Canadian national park, is my favorite place to visit.

2. The painter Vincent Van Gogh cut off part of his ear.

3. The White House, home of the President of the United States, is open to the public for tours.

4. Uncle Marco, my mother's brother, is an engineer.

5. Earth, the only inhabited planet in our solar system, is home to a diverse population of plants and animals.

6. The scorpion, a native of the southwestern part of North America, has a poisonous sting.

7. Emily's prize Persian cat Amelia won first prize at the cat show.

8. Judge Andropov, the presiding judge, sentenced the criminal to prison.

9. Paula's friend from Florida, Luisa, watched a space shuttle launch.

B. Complete each sentence with an appropriate appositive.

1. My friend _____ bought a new bike.

2. The bike, _____, is fast and sleek.

3. Joe and his friend _____ plan to ride their bikes together.

4. They will ride to Pease Park, _____, on Saturday.

5. They plan to meet Anne, _____, on the bike path.

6. After bicycling, they will see a movie, _____.

7. Our friend _____ might come with us.

8. We will get a snack, _____, to eat during the movie.

9. My favorite actor, _____, might be in the movie.

Action Verbs

> - A **verb** is a word that expresses action, being, or state of being.
>   EXAMPLE: Paul **went** to the store.
> - An **action verb** is a verb that expresses action.
>   EXAMPLE: The track star **ran** fast.

■ **Underline the action verb in each sentence.**

1. Watch your favorite television program.
2. Andrea carefully dusted her new piano.
3. Anna, copy the pages carefully.
4. A wood fire burned in the huge fireplace.
5. This button fell from my sweater.
6. The Harlem Globe Trotters play basketball throughout the world.
7. The musicians practiced for the concert.
8. The waves dashed the light craft against the rocks.
9. A sentence expresses a complete thought.
10. Everybody enjoys a good laugh.
11. This long, narrow trail leads to the mountaintop.
12. It snowed almost every day in February.
13. We hiked through the southern part of Arizona.
14. Dan made me a delicious sandwich.
15. Please hand me the salt, Dannette.
16. Draw a line under each verb.
17. We skated on Lake Superior.
18. The woman answered all my questions.
19. The city repaired that pothole last week.
20. Early settlers suffered many hardships.
21. Write your sentence on the board.
22. They moved the car from the street.
23. Thomas Edison often worked eighteen hours a day.
24. Carol directs the community choir.
25. The team played softball all afternoon.
26. We walked along the beach for an hour.
27. Who helped you with your science project?
28. The bridge collapsed.
29. The antique clock ticked loudly.

Linking Verbs

> ■ A **linking verb** does not show action. Instead, it links the subject to a word that either describes the subject or gives the subject another name.
> ■ A verb is a linking verb if it can replace one of the verbs of being (am, is, are, was, were).
>   EXAMPLES: We **were** cold. Nancy **is** a dancer. John **looked** tired.
>   The soup **tastes** delicious.

A. Underline the linking verb in each sentence.

1. Carla appears nervous.

2. She is the first singer on the program.

3. Last year, she was last on the program.

4. Another performer is last this year.

5. The stage looks beautiful.

6. Flowers are everywhere.

7. The flowers smell fresh.

8. Carla feels ready to start.

9. Her song sounds wonderful.

10. The audience seems pleased.

B. Complete each sentence with a linking verb from the box. You may use any verb more than once.

am	appeared	are	became	is	seemed	was	were

1. Tony _____ frightened.

2. He _____ alone in the cabin for the first time.

3. In the dark forest, everything _____ threatening.

4. Because of the storm, the lights _____ out.

5. Even the shadows _____ strange.

6. "This _____ stupid," he thought to himself.

7. "I _____ brave; I'm not a coward."

8. "Where _____ Aaron?" he wondered.

9. There _____ bears in the woods.

10. What if he _____ lost?

Principal Parts of Verbs

- A verb has four principal parts: **present, present participle, past,** and **past participle.**
- For regular verbs, form the present participle by adding -ing to the present. Use a form of the helping verb be with the present participle.
- Form the past and past participle by adding -ed to the present. Use a form of the helping verb have with the past participle.

  EXAMPLES:

Present	Present Participle	Past	Past Participle
laugh	(is) laughing	laughed	(have, has, had) laughed
bake	(is) baking	baked	(have, has, had) baked
live	(is) living	lived	(have, has, had) lived

- Irregular verbs form their past and past participle in other ways. A dictionary shows the principal parts of these verbs.

- **Write the present participle, past, and past participle for each verb.**

PRESENT	PRESENT PARTICIPLE	PAST	PAST PARTICIPLE
1. stop	is stopping	stopped	(have, has, had) stopped
2. listen			
3. carry			
4. help			
5. start			
6. borrow			
7. call			
8. receive			
9. hope			
10. illustrate			
11. divide			
12. change			
13. score			
14. iron			
15. study			
16. collect			
17. laugh			

Verb Phrases

> ■ A **verb phrase** consists of a main verb and one or more **helping verbs.** A helping verb is also called an **auxiliary verb.** In a verb phrase, the helping verb or verbs precede the main verb.   EXAMPLE: James **has arrived.**
> ■ The helping verbs are:
> > am, are, is, was, were, be, being, been
> > has, have, had
> > do, does, did
> > can, could, must, may, might, shall, should, will, would

A. Write a sentence using each word below as the main verb in a verb phrase.

1. gone _____

2. written _____

3. come _____

4. thrown _____

5. draw _____

6. walking _____

7. invent _____

8. sing _____

9. seen _____

10. eaten _____

B. Underline the verb phrase in each sentence.

1. Isabel has returned from a vacation in Florida.

2. She has planned to tell us all about it.

3. Isabel would have answered every question about her trip.

4. Our club officers have been looking for someone to speak.

5. The officers have asked Isabel to the meeting.

6. They have organized an interesting meeting.

7. Every detail of the meeting has been planned carefully.

8. I must speak to Isabel immediately.

9. The lights were dimmed for Isabel's slide show.

10. She said that alligators had been seen in some places.

11. Pets and farm animals were threatened by them.

12. We are planning a trip to Florida next year.

Past Tenses of *See, Go,* and *Begin*

- Never use a helping verb with saw, went, and began.
- Always use a helping verb with seen, gone, and begun.

A. Underline the correct verb.

1. The last person we (saw, seen) in the park was Eric.

2. Who has (went, gone) for the ice?

3. Carla and Yoko (began, begun) to fix the flat tire.

4. Charles (went, gone) to the supermarket for some lettuce.

5. Our summer vacation has (began, begun).

6. They had (saw, seen) a shooting star.

7. Hasn't she (went, gone) to the airport?

8. Yes, we (saw, seen) the concert poster.

9. Alice, have you ever (saw, seen) a penguin?

10. We never (went, gone) to hear the new mayor speak.

11. Olivia, why haven't you (began, begun) your work?

12. Mike (began, begun) to tell us about the accident.

13. Our guests have (went, gone).

14. It (began, begun) to snow early in the evening.

15. Work has finally (began, begun) on the new stadium.

16. We (saw, seen) Pikes Peak last summer.

17. My three sisters (went, gone) to Toronto, Ontario.

18. Have you (saw, seen) the waves pounding the huge boulders?

19. We (went, gone) to hear the symphony last night.

20. They (began, begun) their program with music by Mozart.

21. The program (began, begun) on time.

B. Write a sentence using each verb below.

1. saw _____

2. seen _____

3. gone _____

4. went _____

5. began _____

6. begun _____

Wear, Rise, Steal, Choose, and Break

- Never use a helping verb with <u>wore</u>, <u>rose</u>, <u>stole</u>, <u>chose</u>, and <u>broke</u>.
- Always use a helping verb with <u>worn</u>, <u>risen</u>, <u>stolen</u>, <u>chosen</u>, and <u>broken</u>.

A. Underline the correct verb.

1. We almost froze because we hadn't (wore, worn) coats.

2. Haven't you (chose, chosen) a new shirt?

3. I (broke, broken) my new bike.

4. The river (rose, risen) two feet during the night.

5. Someone had (stole, stolen) our car last week.

6. Juanita had (chose, chosen) many of our old landmarks for the city tour.

7. I have (wore, worn) these uncomfortable shoes for the last time.

8. We were miles along the way when the sun (rose, risen).

9. The squirrels have (stole, stolen) most of our acorns.

10. The airplane (rose, risen) above the clouds.

11. The children have (wore, worn) a path through the backyard.

12. They (chose, chosen) to stay at the camp for a day.

13. Jan had (broke, broken) her leg the summer we visited her.

14. Have you ever (stole, stolen) home base?

15. Our pizza dough had (rose, risen) by the time we sliced the pepperoni.

16. The bottle's protective seal was (broke, broken), so we returned it to the store.

17. Kurt and Jamie (wore, worn) each other's clothes when they were younger.

18. The full moon had (rose, risen) over the deep, dark lake.

19. The jewel thief (stole, stolen) one too many diamonds before he got caught.

B. Circle any mistakes in the use of past tense verbs.

The sun had just rose when Kate recognized the familiar sound of fishing
boats returning to shore. She hadn't meant to sleep late this morning, but the
early morning waves had coaxed her back to sleep. Now, slipping into her
sweatshirt, shoes, and damp shorts, Kate noticed that seagulls had again
stole fish from the pail of bait. She chuckled at the thought, and then tossed
the circling birds another minnow. Turning, Kate noticed Luke nearing the
boat. He worn the same windbreaker and soft, leather shoes nearly every day
since they first met, months ago. Kate paused for a moment. It occurred to
her that she chosen a good friend. Luke had never broke a shoestring, or
a promise.

Come, Ring, Drink, Know, and *Throw*

■ Never use a helping verb with <u>came</u>, <u>rang</u>, <u>drank</u>, <u>knew</u>, and <u>threw</u>.
■ Always use a helping verb with <u>come</u>, <u>rung</u>, <u>drunk</u>, <u>known</u>, and <u>thrown</u>.

A. Underline the correct verb.

1. The tired horse (drank, drunk) from the cool stream.

2. The church bell has not (rang, rung) today.

3. I haven't (drank, drunk) my hot chocolate.

4. We (knew, known) that it was time to go.

5. Have you (threw, thrown) the garbage out?

6. Haven't the movers (came, come) for our furniture?

7. We (rang, rung) the fire alarm five minutes ago.

8. Haven't you (know, known) him for a long time?

9. I (threw, thrown) the ball to James.

10. My friends from London, England, (came, come) this afternoon.

11. Why haven't you (drank, drunk) your juice?

12. I always (came, come) to work in my wheelchair now.

13. I (knew, known) Pat when she was just a child.

14. Have you (threw, thrown) away last week's newspaper?

15. We have (came, come) to tell you something.

16. If you already (rang, rung) the bell, then you might try knocking.

17. Tony thinks he (drank, drunk) something that made him ill.

B. Write a sentence using each verb below.

1. came _____

2. come _____

3. rang _____

4. rung _____

5. threw _____

6. thrown _____

7. drank _____

8. drunk _____

9. knew _____

Eat, Fall, Draw, Drive, and Run

- Never use a helping verb with <u>ate</u>, <u>fell</u>, <u>drew</u>, <u>drove</u>, and <u>ran</u>.
- Always use a helping verb with <u>eaten</u>, <u>fallen</u>, <u>drawn</u>, <u>driven</u>, and <u>run</u>.

A. Underline the correct verb.

1. Taro, have you (drew, drawn) your diagram?

2. When we had (drove, driven) for two hours, we (began, begun) to feel hungry.

3. All of our pears have (fell, fallen) from the tree.

4. After we had (ate, eaten) our dinner, we (ran, run) around the lake.

5. A great architect (drew, drawn) the plans for our civic center.

6. We had just (ran, run) into the house when we saw our friends.

7. Hadn't the building already (fell, fallen) when you (ran, run) around the corner?

8. Those heavy curtains in the theater have (fell, fallen) down.

9. Last week we (drove, driven) to the lake for a vacation.

10. I have just (ate, eaten) a delicious slice of pizza.

11. I (ate, eaten) my breakfast before six o'clock this morning.

12. All of the leaves have (fell, fallen) from the elm trees.

13. When was the last time you (ran, run) a mile?

B. Write the correct past tense form of each verb in parentheses to complete the sentences.

1. (drive)   Last weekend we _____ to the lake for a picnic.

2. (draw)   Since Jenna knew several shortcuts, she _____ a detailed map for us.

3. (fall)   She mentioned that during a recent summer storm, debris had _____ on many of the roads.

4. (fall)   She warned us that a large tree _____ on one of the main roads.

5. (drive)   Jenna claimed that she had never _____ under such dangerous circumstances.

6. (run)   "I almost _____ right into that tree in the dark!" Jenna said.

7. (eat)   In order to avoid traveling at night, we _____ our dinner after we got home from the lake.

8. (eat)   We had _____ so much during our picnic that none of us minded waiting!

9. (draw)   Once home, we all agreed that Jenna had _____ a great map for us.

10. (run)   We made the trip in record time, and we hadn't _____ over any trees in the process!

Forms of *Do*

- Never use a helping verb with did.
  - EXAMPLE: Anne **did** a great job on her test.
- Always use a helping verb with done.
  - EXAMPLE: Hallie **had** also **done** a great job.
- Doesn't is the contraction of does not. Use it with singular nouns and the pronouns he, she, and it.
  - EXAMPLES: Rachel **doesn't** want to go. It **doesn't** seem right.
- Don't is the contraction of do not. Use it with plural nouns and with the pronouns I, you, we, and they.
  - EXAMPLES: Mr. and Mrs. Ricci **don't** live there. You **don't** have your purse.

A. Underline the correct verb.

1. Why (doesn't, don't) Lois have the car keys?

2. Show me the way you (did, done) it.

3. Have the three of you (did, done) most of the work?

4. Why (doesn't, don't) she cash a check today?

5. Please show me what damage the storm (did, done).

6. (Doesn't, Don't) the workers on the morning shift do a fine job?

7. Have the new owners of our building (did, done) anything about the plumbing?

8. (Doesn't, Don't) those apples look overly ripe?

9. Chris (doesn't, don't) want to do the spring cleaning this week.

10. The gloves and the hat (doesn't, don't) match.

11. Carolyn, have you (did, done) your homework today?

12. Who (did, done) this fine job of painting?

13. (Doesn't, Don't) the tile in our new kitchen look nice?

14. (Doesn't, Don't) that dog stay in a fenced yard?

15. He has (did, done) me a great favor.

16. I will help if he (doesn't, don't).

B. Write one sentence using did and one sentence using done.

1. _____

2. _____

C. Write one sentence using doesn't and one sentence using don't.

1. _____

2. _____

Transitive and Intransitive Verbs

> ■ There are two kinds of action verbs: **transitive** and **intransitive**.
> ■ A transitive verb has a direct object.
>   D.O.
>   EXAMPLE: Jeffrey **painted** the house.
> ■ An intransitive verb does not need an object to complete its meaning.
>   EXAMPLES: The sun **rises** in the east. She **walks** quickly.

A. Underline the verb in each sentence. Then write T for transitive or I for intransitive.

_____ **1.** Kristina joined the health club in March.

_____ **2.** She wanted the exercise to help her stay healthy.

_____ **3.** Kristina exercised every day after work.

_____ **4.** She became friends with Nancy.

_____ **5.** They worked out together.

_____ **6.** Nancy preferred the treadmill.

_____ **7.** Kristina liked aerobics and running.

_____ **8.** Sometimes they switched activities.

_____ **9.** Nancy took an aerobics class.

_____ **10.** Kristina used the treadmill.

_____ **11.** Occasionally they swam in the pool.

_____ **12.** Nancy was the better swimmer.

_____ **13.** But Kristina had more fun.

_____ **14.** She just splashed around in the water.

B. Underline the transitive verb, and circle the direct object in each sentence.

1. Carlos walked Tiny every day.

2. Tiny usually pulled Carlos along.

3. Carlos washed Tiny every other week.

4. Tiny loved water.

5. He splashed Carlos whenever he could.

6. Tiny also loved rawhide bones.

7. He chewed the bones until they were gone.

8. Carlos found Tiny when Tiny was just a puppy.

Verbals

- A **verbal** is a verb form that functions as a noun or adjective. There are three types of verbals: **infinitives, participles,** and **gerunds.**
- An **infinitive** is the base form of the verb, commonly preceded by <u>to</u>. An infinitive that functions as a noun is a verbal.
  - EXAMPLE: The object of the game is **to win.**
- A present or past **participle** that functions as an adjective is a verbal.
  - EXAMPLES: A **running** horse galloped down the road. **Dried** leaves flew from his hooves.
- A **gerund** is the present participle of a verb form ending in <u>-ing</u> that is used as a noun.
  - EXAMPLE: **Skiing** is her favorite sport.

A. Underline the infinitive in each sentence below.

1. Alan refused to quit.

2. The only thing he wanted was to finish.

3. Alan had trained to run this race for months.

4. It was not important to win.

5. Alan simply needed to finish.

6. He hoped to accomplish his goal.

7. Soon he was close enough to see the finish line.

B. Underline the participle in each sentence below.

1. A yelling cheerleader led the crowd.

2. The excited crowd roared.

3. The running team took the field.

4. The marching band started to play.

5. Chosen members of the band flashed cards.

6. The flashing cards spelled a message.

7. The interested students studied hard.

C. Underline the gerund in each sentence below.

1. Studying is an important job.

2. Language arts and reading help improve your language ability.

3. Learning can be rewarding.

4. Memorizing is another skill you can learn.

5. Remembering is not always easy.

6. Do you think studying is time well spent?

7. Dancing is Lauren's favorite activity.

D. Underline the verbal in each sentence, and write <u>infinitive</u>, <u>participle</u>, or <u>gerund</u> on the line.

_____ 1. To act in a play is an honor.

_____ 2. Acting can be very exciting.

_____ 3. To write plays takes a lot of skill.

_____ 4. Working in the theater is interesting.

_____ 5. Sally wanted to participate.

_____ 6. The hurried director got ready for the auditions.

_____ 7. Sally prepared a moving scene.

_____ 8. She was finally ready to read her scene.

_____ 9. Auditioning can scare anyone.

_____ 10. Sally's stirring performance won her a part.

_____ 11. Rehearsing can take up much time.

_____ 12. The actors must work long hours to memorize their parts.

_____ 13. Sally's convincing performance was outstanding.

_____ 14. All of the actors excelled in performing.

_____ 15. The smiling director congratulated the cast.

_____ 16. "To act is an art," said the director.

_____ 17. He called them all budding artists.

_____ 18. Performing is a pleasure for Yolanda.

_____ 19. Bowing is even more fun.

_____ 20. The audience could tell by Yolanda's face that she enjoyed

playing the part.

_____ 21. To continue her studies is her goal.

_____ 22. Acting is very important to Yolanda and Sally.

_____ 23. Interrupted lessons would distress them both.

_____ 24. They are consumed with acting.

_____ 25. They need constant practice to excel.

_____ 26. Well-rehearsed actors perform better.

Active and Passive Voice

- **Voice** refers to the relation of a subject to its verb.
- In the **active voice,** the subject acts.
  EXAMPLE: **I painted** the house.
- In the **passive voice,** the subject receives the action.
  EXAMPLE: The house **was painted** by me.
- Only transitive verbs are used in the passive voice.

A. Write A if the sentence is in the active voice and P if it is in the passive voice.

_____ 1. Marty applied for a job in a grocery store.

_____ 2. He needs money for gas and car repairs.

_____ 3. He will handle the cash register.

_____ 4. Marty will also stock the shelves.

_____ 5. The application was turned in last week.

_____ 6. The store's manager reads every application.

_____ 7. Then the applicants are interviewed.

_____ 8. Marty was interviewed on Monday.

_____ 9. The manager was impressed by Marty.

_____ 10. He will give Marty the job.

B. Rewrite each sentence in the active voice.

1. Kate was given a job babysitting by the McNeils.

_____

2. The children will be watched by her every day.

_____

3. Kate will be driven to their house by her friend.

_____

C. Rewrite each sentence in the passive voice.

1. Trina plays the drums in the band.

_____

2. She chose the drums because her father played drums.

_____

3. Trina won an award for her playing.

_____

Pronouns

- A **subject pronoun** is used in the subject of a sentence and after a linking verb.
  - EXAMPLES: **We** are going to the tournament. The woman in the suit is **she.**
- An **object pronoun** is used after an action verb or a preposition.
  - EXAMPLE: James threw the ball to **me.**
- A **possessive pronoun** is used to show ownership of something.
  - EXAMPLES: The red shoes are **mine.** Those are **my** red shoes.
- An **indefinite pronoun** does not refer to a specific person or thing.
  - EXAMPLE: **Someone** should take that history class.
- Use <u>who</u> as a subject pronoun, and use <u>whom</u> as an object pronoun.
  - EXAMPLES: **Who** is going to the party? We will ask **whom** to go with us?

A. Underline each correct pronoun.

1. Stephanie spoke to Jennifer and (I, me) about it.

2. Dean sent Tom and (they, them) some new shirts.

3. Please bring Anne and (I, me) some cool water.

4. Here comes (my, me) brother David.

5. Susan and (he, him) were late today.

6. Was it (she, her) who answered the knock?

7. I don't believe it was (they, them)!

8. Mona took Doug and (we, us) to work.

9. He told Steven and (she, her) about the problem.

10. Don't you think (someone, us) should help?

11. Rosa and (I, me) are going to work until seven o'clock.

12. It wasn't (your, yours) cat that meowed.

13. (He, Him) and Calvin are going to the game.

14. She told Kate and (my, me) about her fishing trip.

15. (Who, Whom) did you say got here early?

16. He said that it was (they, them) who came to our house.

17. (Everyone, We) will carry his or her own bundles.

18. It was (they, their) babysitter who knocked on the door.

19. (Who, Whom) did you meet for lunch?

20. Elizabeth and (she, her) always sit together.

21. This sweater is (hers, she).

22. (Who, Whom) led the band in the parade?

23. The red car is (our, ours).

24. Can you predict (who, whom) will win the election?

B. Underline each pronoun.

1. I told you to speak to him about our fishing trip.

2. Who is speaking?

3. They saw us when we passed by their house.

4. Just between you and me, I want to go with them.

5. He and Mike are going with us.

6. My decision to leave was made before our conversation.

7. Whom did you see?

8. This package was sent to you and me.

9. They are going with us to the game.

10. Jerry broke his arm.

11. Who told them?

12. She is my friend who moved to Mexico.

13. This check is mine.

14. Someone took some fresh flowers to them.

15. Who is she?

16. She went with us to the parade.

17. John, who is the president of that company?

18. Will she go with you?

19. Who telephoned me?

20. Should we eat with them at the picnic?

21. Which is your raincoat?

22. Did I tell you about our plans?

23. Which is mine?

24. Do you recall your sister's middle initial?

25. Why can't you come with us?

26. Did anybody get a letter?

27. You and I are on the list, too.

28. Did you see him?

C. Write sentences using the following pronouns:

1. theirs _____

2. you and I _____

3. you and me _____

4. them _____

5. anyone _____

Antecedents

- An **antecedent** is the word to which a pronoun refers.
  - EXAMPLE: **Dogs** are dangerous if **they** bite.
- A pronoun must agree with its antecedent in **gender, (masculine, feminine,** or **neuter)** and in **number** (singular or plural).
  - EXAMPLES: **Sally** washed **her** hair. The **storm** changed **its** course. The **workers** went to **their** offices.
- If the antecedent is an indefinite pronoun (one that doesn't refer to a specific person or thing), it is correct to use a masculine pronoun. However, it is now common to use both a masculine and a feminine pronoun.
  - EXAMPLES: **Someone** lost **his** gloves. **Someone** lost **his or her** gloves.

A. Underline each pronoun. Circle its antecedent.

1. Mike said he would tutor Carmen.

2. Carmen was doing poorly in her math class.

3. Carmen often shakes her head in confusion.

4. Mike promised to try his hardest.

5. Carmen worked on her math, but it was difficult.

6. Mike and Carmen said they would work every night.

7. The math test was coming, and it promised to be hard.

8. The class was ready for its test.

9. Carmen's palms were sweaty, and they felt clammy.

10. The teacher said he knew Carmen would do well.

11. When Carmen started the test, it didn't seem so hard.

12. Each student finished his or her test and put it on the instructor's desk.

13. The instructor would correct the tests and hand them back.

14. Carmen was pleased with her grade.

B. Circle the pronoun in parentheses that agrees with the antecedent.

1. Earl and Leon practiced (their, his) free throws.

2. Each hoped practice would make (him, her) play better.

3. The team held (its, their) practice every day.

4. Leon practiced (his, their) passing.

5. It is important to study the plays because (they, he) must be remembered.

6. Carl waxed (him, his) car.

7. The building was closed because (its, their) windows were damaged in the storm.

8. The flowers opened (its, their) petals in the sunshine.

9. Maggie found (his, her) book in the closet.

10. The guests piled (their, them) coats on the table.

Adjectives

- An **adjective** is a word that modifies a noun or a pronoun.
  - EXAMPLE: He likes **chocolate** cookies.
- Adjectives usually tell **what kind, which one,** or **how many.**
  - EXAMPLES: **bright** penny, **these** oranges, **twelve** classmates
- A **proper adjective** is an adjective that is formed from a proper noun. It always begins with a capital letter.
  - EXAMPLES: **Asian** continent, **English** language
- The articles a, an, and the are called **limiting adjectives.**

A. Write three adjectives to describe each noun.

1. mountains _____ _____ _____

2. weather _____ _____ _____

3. journey _____ _____ _____

4. classroom _____ _____ _____

5. book _____ _____ _____

B. Underline each adjective.

1. This old chair is comfortable.

2. We have read a funny story recently.

3. This heavy traffic creates many dangerous situations.

4. The eager sailors collected odd souvenirs at every port.

5. The tired, thirsty soldiers marched on.

6. This is my favorite book.

7. The solitary guard walked along the lonely beach.

8. We sat in the sixth row.

9. These damp matches will not strike.

10. Dan made French toast for breakfast.

11. Will you light those candles, please?

12. A red bird chirped loudly in the tall tree.

13. The heavy elephant sat down slowly.

14. A tour bus stopped at the pirate's cove.

15. The gorgeous model wore Italian leather.

16. We ate fresh seafood on our vacation.

17. Do you like mashed or baked potatoes?

18. She served Chinese food for dinner.

Demonstrative Adjectives

> - A **demonstrative adjective** is one that points out a specific person or thing.
> - <u>This</u> and <u>that</u> modify singular nouns. <u>This</u> points to a person or thing nearby, and <u>that</u> points to a person or thing farther away.
>   EXAMPLES: **This** movie is my favorite. **That** sign is difficult to see.
> - <u>These</u> and <u>those</u> modify plural nouns. <u>These</u> points to persons or things nearby and <u>those</u> points to persons or things farther away.
>   EXAMPLES: **These** ribbons are the most colorful.
>   **Those** towels need to be folded.
> - The word <u>them</u> is a pronoun. Never use it to describe a noun.

- **Underline the correct demonstrative adjective.**

1. Move (those, them) plants inside since it may freeze tonight.

2. (These, That) box in front of me is too heavy to lift.

3. Who brought us (those, them) delicious cookies?

4. Look at (those, them) playful kittens.

5. (That, Those) kind of friend is appreciated.

6. (Those, Them) pictures are beautiful.

7. What are (those, them) sounds I hear?

8. Did you ever meet (those, them) people?

9. We have just developed (these, them) photographs.

10. Do you know any of (those, them) young people?

11. May we take some of (these, them) folders?

12. I have been looking over (these, them) magazines.

13. Do not eat too many of (those, them) peaches.

14. I do not like (this, these) kind of syrup.

15. (Those, Them) people should be served next.

16. Jimmy, please mail (these, them) letters.

17. Look at (those, them) posters I made!

18. (This, That) suburb is fifty miles away.

19. (These, Them) antique coins are valuable.

20. Look at (those, that) soccer players hustle!

21. José, may we see (these, them) photographs?

22. Please return (that, these) library books.

23. (These, Them) clothes need to be washed.

24. Please hand me (that, those) plates.

25. (Those, Them) cookies have nuts in them.

Comparing with Adjectives

- An adjective has three degrees of comparison: **positive, comparative,** and **superlative.**
- The simple form of the adjective is called the **positive** degree.
    - EXAMPLE: Ian is **short.**
- When two people or things are being compared, the **comparative** degree is used.
    - EXAMPLE: Ian is **shorter** than Lee.
- When three or more people or things are being compared, the **superlative** degree is used.
    - EXAMPLE: Ian is the **shortest** person in the group.
- For all adjectives of one syllable and a few adjectives of two syllables, add -er to form the comparative degree, and -est to form the superlative degree.
    - EXAMPLE: smart—smarter—smartest
- For some adjectives of two syllables and all adjectives of three or more syllables, use more or less to form the comparative and most or least to form the superlative.
    - EXAMPLES: This test is **more** difficult than I expected. Carol is the **most** generous of all. Kate is **less** talkative than Tom. Mary is the **least** talkative of all.

- **Complete each sentence with the correct degree of comparison of the adjective given in parentheses. Some of the forms are irregular.**

1. (changeable) The weather seems _____ this year than last.

2. (faithful) I think the dog is the _____ of all animals.

3. (agreeable) Is James _____ than Sam?

4. (busy) Theresa is the _____ person in the office.

5. (long) Which is the _____ river, the Mississippi or the **Amazon?**

6. (lovely) I think the rose is the _____ of all flowers.

7. (fresh) Show me the _____ cookies in the store.

8. (high) Which of the two mountains is _____?

9. (enjoyable) Which is the _____, television or the **movies?**

10. (reckless) That person is the _____ driver in town.

11. (young) Of all the players, Maria is the _____.

12. (tall) Alberto is the _____ of the three men.

13. (difficult) Isn't the seventh problem _____ than the eighth?

14. (quiet) We have found the _____ spot in the park.

Adverbs

- An **adverb** is a word that modifies a verb, an adjective, or another adverb.
  EXAMPLES: The rain poured **steadily.** His memories were **extremely** vivid. She responded **very** quickly.
- An adverb usually tells **how, when, where,** or **how often.**
- Many adverbs end in -<u>ly</u>.

A. Underline each adverb.

1. The person read slowly but clearly and expressively.

2. Adam, you are driving too recklessly.

3. The airplane started moving slowly but quickly gained speed.

4. I spoke too harshly to my friends.

5. How did all of you get here?

6. I looked everywhere for my pen.

7. The man stopped suddenly and quickly turned around.

8. Stacy read that poem too rapidly.

9. Janice plays the guitar well.

10. The child was sleeping soundly.

11. The car was running noisily.

12. We returned early.

13. Those trees were severely damaged in the fire.

14. Jack ran quickly, but steadily, in the race.

B. Write two adverbs that could be used to modify each verb.

1. read _____ _____

2. think _____ _____

3. walk _____ _____

4. eat _____ _____

5. sing _____ _____

6. speak _____ _____

7. dive _____ _____

8. study _____ _____

9. write _____ _____

10. look _____ _____

Comparing with Adverbs

- An **adverb** has three degrees of comparison: **positive, comparative,** and **superlative.**
- The simple form of the adverb is called the **positive** degree.
  EXAMPLE: Kathy ran **fast** in the race.
- When two actions are being compared, the **comparative** degree is used.
  EXAMPLE: Amy ran **faster** than Kathy.
- When three or more actions are being compared, the **superlative** degree is used.
  EXAMPLE: Maureen ran the **fastest** of all.
- Use -er to form the comparative degree and use -est to form the superlative degree of one-syllable adverbs.
- Use more or most with longer adverbs and with adverbs that end in -ly.
  EXAMPLES: Louisa ran **more energetically** than Bob.
  Ms. Baker ran the **most energetically** of all the runners.

A. **Underline the adverb that best completes each sentence.**

1. Mark arrived (sooner, soonest) than Greg.

2. Tony arrived the (sooner, soonest) of all.

3. They had to work very (hard, harder, hardest).

4. Tony painted (more, most) carefully than Mark.

5. Mark worked (faster, fastest) than Greg, so Mark painted the walls.

6. Lauren worked the (more, most) carefully of all.

B. **Complete each sentence with the proper form of the adverb in parentheses.**

1. (fast)   Jason wanted to be the _____ runner at our school.

2. (fast)   Juan could run _____ than Jason.

3. (seriously)   Jason trained _____ than he had before.

4. (frequently)   Jason is on the track _____ of all the runners.

5. (quickly)   Jason ran the sprint _____ than he did yesterday.

6. (promptly)   Jason arrives for practice _____ of anyone on the team.

7. (promptly)   He even arrives _____ than the coach!

8. (eagerly)   Juan does warm-up exercises _____ of all the runners.

9. (carefully)   Who concentrates _____ on his timing, Juan or Jason?

10. (hard)   The coach congratulates Jason on being the player who works the

_____.

Prepositions

> - A **preposition** is a word that shows the relationship of a noun or a pronoun to another word in the sentence.
>   EXAMPLES: The child ran **into** the **house.** He put his boots **under** the **table.**
> - These are some commonly used prepositions:
> | about | against | at | between | from | of | through | under |
> | above | among | behind | by | in | on | to | upon |
> | across | around | beside | for | into | over | toward | with |

- **Underline each preposition in the sentences below.**

1. Can you draw a map of your area?

2. Who is the owner of this car?

3. The pecan is a common tree in the South.

4. For whom are you waiting?

5. At the meeting, he spoke to me about your athletic ability.

6. Our company is proud of its industrious employees.

7. Her friend Cynthia stood beside her.

8. A small amount of that soup is all I want.

9. We went to the house at the end of the street.

10. There were seventy-five post offices in the United States in 1790.

11. Most of the spectators stood during the last quarter of the game.

12. These shoes of mine are too tight at the heel.

13. We ate dinner at the new restaurant near the river.

14. They stood on the porch and watched for the mail carrier.

15. Anyone can succeed with hard work.

16. We walked behind that group.

17. Astronaut Sally Ride was the first woman in space.

18. A group of people on horses rode behind the band.

19. We walked to the picnic grounds during the lunch hour.

20. Ben slid down the slippery hill.

21. There is a bridge across the river in our town.

22. The ball was knocked over the fence and into the pond.

23. I see a spot of dirt under your left eye.

24. One can observe a strange world below the surface of an ocean.

25. The rocket quickly disappeared behind the clouds.

26. Much of our land is drained by the Mississippi River.

27. Please sit between us.

28. This package is for you.

Prepositional Phrases

- A **phrase** is a group of closely related words used as a single part of speech but not containing a subject and predicate.
  - EXAMPLE: The writer **of this novel** is signing autographs.
- A **prepositional phrase** is a group of words that begins with a preposition and ends with a noun or pronoun.
  - EXAMPLE: He took the train **to New York.**
- The noun or pronoun in the prepositional phrase is called the **object of the preposition.**
  - EXAMPLE: He took the train to **New York.**

- **Put parentheses around each prepositional phrase. Then underline each preposition, and circle the object of the preposition.**

  1. The airplane was flying (above the (clouds)).
  2. We are moving to North Carolina.
  3. Sandra lives on the second block.
  4. An old water tower once stood on that hill.
  5. The car slid on the wet pavement.
  6. Sealing wax was invented in the seventeenth century.
  7. Motto rings were first used by the Romans.
  8. Tungsten, a metal, was discovered in 1781.
  9. Roses originally came from Asia.
  10. The ball rolled into the street.
  11. Do you always keep the puppies in a pen?
  12. The children climbed over the fence.
  13. She lives in Denver, Colorado.
  14. Columbus made three trips to North America.
  15. They spread the lunch under the shade of the giant elm tree.
  16. The treasure was found by a scuba diver.
  17. A squad of soldiers marched behind the tank.
  18. Shall I row across the stream?
  19. Large airplanes fly across the nation.
  20. Walter looked into the sack.
  21. The cat ran up the pole.
  22. We visited the Alexander Graham Bell Museum in Nova Scotia.
  23. Many tourists come to our region.
  24. We spent last summer in the Adirondack Mountains.
  25. Do not stand behind a parked car.

Prepositional Phrases as Adjectives and Adverbs

> ■ A prepositional phrase can be used to describe a noun or a pronoun.
> Then the prepositional phrase is being used as an **adjective** to tell
> which one, what kind, or how many.
>   EXAMPLE: The bird **in the tree** whistled.
>   The prepositional phrase <u>in the tree</u> tells **which** bird.
> ■ A prepositional phrase can be used to describe a verb. Then the prepositional
> phrase is being used as an **adverb** to tell how, where, or when.
>   EXAMPLE: Charlie ate breakfast **before leaving for school.**
>   The prepositional phrase **before leaving for school** tells **when**
>   Charlie ate breakfast.

■ **Underline each prepositional phrase, and classify it as adjective or adverb.**

 1. They went <u>to the ranch</u>. *adv.*

 2. The first savings bank was established in France.

 3. Fall Creek Falls in Tennessee is my home.

 4. Return all books to the public library.

 5. Mark lives in an old house.

 6. Tanya bought a sweater with red trim.

 7. The birds in the zoo are magnificent.

 8. Jade is found in Burma.

 9. I spent the remainder of my money.

10. The magician waved a wand over the hat, and a rabbit appeared.

11. The diameter of a Sequoia tree trunk can reach ten feet.

12. The capital of New York is Albany.

13. The narrowest streets are near the docks.

14. Our family went to the movie.

15. Roald Amundsen discovered the South Pole in 1911.

16. The floor in this room is painted black.

17. The dead leaves are blowing across the yard.

18. A forest of petrified wood has been found.

19. The mole's tunnel runs across the lawn.

Conjunctions

> - A **conjunction** is a word used to join words or groups of words.
>   EXAMPLES: Yuri **and** Brant have arrived. They worked **until** the sun went down.
> - These are some commonly used conjunctions:
>
> | although | because | however | or | that | when | whereas |
> |----------|---------|---------|-----|------|------|---------|
> | and | but | if | since | though | whether | yet |
> | as | for | nor | than | unless | while | |
>
> - Some conjunctions are used in pairs. These include either . . . or, neither . . . nor, and not only . . . but also.

■ **Underline each conjunction in the sentences below.**

1. Do you know whether Brandon is going to the employment office?

2. Jesse, are you and Ryan going to see a movie this afternoon?

3. Linda will go to the coast when the weather turns warm.

4. Gina or Vicki will take me to practice.

5. Are you and Elizabeth going swimming this Saturday?

6. Paul will be here unless he has to work.

7. Dean or I must go to the supermarket.

8. Chicken and potatoes are my favorite foods.

9. The trainer and the animals gave a good show.

10. I was angry at Megan because she was not on time.

11. Tom gets into trouble, but he usually gets out of it.

12. Carelessness is the cause of many falls and burns.

13. She stopped work because she had to leave early.

14. Matt has been understanding since I started working two jobs.

15. This chair is small, but it is comfortable.

16. Although it looked like rain, we went for a drive.

17. Kerry is two years older than Tom.

18. The remark was neither just nor kind.

19. You may go either by bus or by plane.

20. Tim is here, but he is too busy to help us right now.

21. Let's go inside, for it is getting dark.

22. We listened closely while the directions were given.

23. Fruit is not only delicious, but also healthful.

24. Bring either a short poem or a rhyme to class tomorrow.

25. Anne neither asked for help nor received any.

26. Neither Joe nor Marie went to the show.

Unit 3 Test

Choose the type of noun underlined in each sentence.

1. <u>Alaska</u> is a cold and icy state.   **A** ○ common   **B** ○ proper

2. Its <u>land</u> has sparse vegetation.   **A** ○ common   **B** ○ proper

3. <u>Glaciers</u> hold much fresh water.   **A** ○ common   **B** ○ proper

4. <u>Alaska's</u> wildlife has adapted to the cold.   **A** ○ common   **B** ○ proper

Choose the correct plural form of each underlined noun.

5. <u>half</u>
   - **A** ○ halves
   - **B** ○ halfs
   - **C** ○ halfes

6. <u>piano</u>
   - **A** ○ pianoes
   - **B** ○ piano's
   - **C** ○ pianos

7. <u>brush</u>
   - **A** ○ brushes
   - **B** ○ brushs
   - **C** ○ brush's

Choose the sentences that contain an appositive or an appositive phrase.

8. **A** ○ Although we were tired, we were happy.
   B ○ After Carmen left, the rest of us played a game.
   C ○ Hearts, the game we chose, is a card game.
   D ○ As usual, Erica won.

9. **A** ○ Craig, an artist, drew my picture.
   B ○ He asked my friend to pose next.
   C ○ After he finished, he gave us the drawings.
   D ○ They were funny cartoons of us, and we laughed.

Choose the correct verb or verb phrase to complete each sentence.

10. This trail _____ to the park ranger's outpost.   **A** ○ leads   **B** ○ has lead   **C** ○ is led

11. The first thing we _____ was clean up.   **A** ○ do   **B** ○ did   **C** ○ done

12. I know you _____ that movie already.   **A** ○ have seen   **B** ○ see   **C** ○ are seeing

13. Suddenly it _____ to rain heavily.   **A** ○ begun   **B** ○ began   **C** ○ begin

14. They _____ before the sun.   **A** ○ rising   **B** ○ risen   **C** ○ rose

15. Haven't you _____ your tea?   **A** ○ drank   **B** ○ drinking   **C** ○ drunk

16. I had _____ out of gas.   **A** ○ run   **B** ○ ran   **C** ○ running

17. He _____ his own car.   **A** ○ drove   **B** ○ drive   **C** ○ driven

Choose the sentence that contains an infinitive, a participle, or a gerund.

18. **A** ○ I swam this afternoon.
    B ○ Are you going to today's race?
    C ○ Dancing is a good form of exercise.

19. **A** ○ The leaves had fallen off the tree.
    B ○ I wasn't going to the party.
    C ○ I hope to win a scholarship for college.

Choose the sentence in which the pronoun agrees with its antecedent.

20. **A** ○ Both boys wrote his editorial for the paper.

    B ○ The topic was chosen because of their relevance.

    C ○ The paper printed both letters in its opinion section.

Choose the correct pronoun to complete each sentence.

21. Have you seen ___ new houses?   **A** ○ these   **B** ○ them   **C** ○ that   **D** ○ this

22. ___ and Pat will debate today.   **A** ○ She   **B** ○ Them   **C** ○ Her   **D** ○ Us

23. You gave the prize to ___ ?   **A** ○ who   **B** ○ she   **C** ○ whom   **D** ○ they

24. Isabel already showed ___ her pictures.   **A** ○ them   **B** ○ they   **C** ○ I   **D** ○ she

25. Joan rode with Mark and ___.   **A** ○ she   **B** ○ I   **C** ○ we   **D** ○ me

26. He told Alex's and ___ parents.   **A** ○ mine   **B** ○ my   **C** ○ us   **D** ○ hers

27. ___ needs to fix that.   **A** ○ We   **B** ○ They   **C** ○ Someone   **D** ○ I

28. The black dog is ___.   **A** ○ ours   **B** ○ our   **C** ○ she   **D** ○ their

Choose the correct form of the adjective or adverb to complete each sentence.

29. These are the ___ cookies I've ever tasted.   **A** ○ delicious   **B** ○ most delicious   **C** ○ more delicious

30. We left ___ than Ling did to avoid the traffic.   **A** ○ earlier   **B** ○ earliest   **C** ○ more early

31. She wanted to read a ___ book than her last one.   **A** ○ funny   **B** ○ funnier   **C** ○ funniest

32. The new heater runs ___ than our old one.   **A** ○ most efficiently   **B** ○ efficiently   **C** ○ more efficiently

33. Walnut and Elm are the ___ streets in the city.   **A** ○ busiest   **B** ○ busy   **C** ○ busier

34. French is ___ to learn than Spanish.   **A** ○ most difficult   **B** ○ difficult   **C** ○ more difficult

Choose whether each underlined group of words is (A) a prepositional phrase used as an adjective, (B) a prepositional phrase used as an adverb, or (C) not a prepositional phrase.

35. I spent my two-week vacation in Brazil.   **A** ○   **B** ○   **C** ○

36. We saw almost every kind of tropical animal.   **A** ○   **B** ○   **C** ○

37. I met a family from Spain.   **A** ○   **B** ○   **C** ○

38. They told me about the language differences.   **A** ○   **B** ○   **C** ○

39. Portuguese and Spanish only sound similar.   **A** ○   **B** ○   **C** ○

Choose the conjunction or conjunctions in each sentence.

40. Salad is not only good, but good for you.   **A** ○ only   **B** ○ for   **C** ○ not only...but

41. Eating green and yellow vegetables can help you stay healthy.   **A** ○ can   **B** ○ and   **C** ○ you

42. Kamal was mad because I was so late.   **A** ○ because   **B** ○ so   **C** ○ late

Using Capital Letters

- **Capitalize** the first word of a sentence and of each line of poetry.
  EXAMPLES: Jim recited a poem. The first two lines follow.
  All the animals looked up in wonder
  When they heard the roaring thunder.
- Capitalize the first word of a direct quotation.
  EXAMPLE: Beth said, "Let's try to memorize a poem, too."
- Capitalize the first, last, and all important words in the titles of books, poems, stories, and songs.
  EXAMPLES: *The Jungle Book,* "Snow Time"

A. Circle each letter that should be capitalized. Write the capital letter above it.

1. Anthony said, "what time does the movie start?"

2. francis Scott Key wrote "the star spangled banner."

3. edgar Allan Poe, the author of "the raven," was born in Boston.

4. paul asked, "when do you plan to visit your friend?"

5. who wrote the poems "snowbound" and "the barefoot boy"?

6. what famous American said, "give me liberty, or give me death"?

- Capitalize all **proper nouns.**
  EXAMPLES: James T. White, Mother, Fifth Avenue, Italy, Missouri
  Smokey Mountains, Thanksgiving, November, Statue of Liberty,
  Mayflower, British Columbia
- Capitalize all **proper adjectives.** A proper adjective is an adjective that is made from a proper noun.
  EXAMPLES: the Italian language, Chinese food, French tourists

B. Circle each letter that should be capitalized. Write the capital letter above it.

1. Lauren, does your friend live in miami, florida, or atlanta, georgia?

2. The potomac river forms the boundary between virginia and maryland.

3. The *pinta,* the *niña,* and the *santa maría* were the ships columbus sailed.

4. The spanish explorers discovered the mississippi river before the english settlers

   landed at jamestown.

5. The founder of the american red cross was clara barton.

6. Glaciers are found in the rocky mountains, the andes mountains, and the alps.

> ■ Capitalize a person's title when it comes before a name.
>   EXAMPLES: Mayor Flynn, Doctor Suarez, Governor Kuhn
> ■ Capitalize abbreviations of titles.
>   EXAMPLES: Ms. C. Cooke, Dr. Pearsoll, Gov. Milne, Judge Brenner

C. Circle each letter that should be capitalized. Write the capital letter above it.

1. How long have you been seeing dr. thompson?

2. Our class invited mayor thomas to speak at graduation.

3. dr. crawford w. long of Georgia is believed to be the first physician to

use ether during surgery.

4. What time do you expect mr. and mrs. randall to arrive?

5. Most people believe senator dixon will win reelection.

6. It will be a close election unless gov. alden gives his support.

7. When is ms. howell scheduled to begin teaching?

> ■ Capitalize abbreviations of days and months, parts of addresses, and
>   titles of members of the armed forces. Also capitalize all letters in the
>   abbreviations of states.
>   EXAMPLES: Tues.; Nov.; 201 S. Main St.; Maj. Donna C. Plunkett;
>   Boston, MA

D. Circle each letter that should be capitalized. Write the capital letter above it.

1. niles school art fair

sat., feb. 8th, 9 A.M.

110 n. elm dr.

2. shoreville water festival

june 23–24

mirror lake

shoreville, mn 55108

3. october fest

october 28 and 29

9 A.M.–5 P.M.

63 maple st.

4. barbara dumont

150 telson rd.

markham, ontario L3R 1E5

5. captain c. j. neil

c/o *ocean star*

p.o. box 4455

portsmouth, nh 03801

6. dr. charles b. stevens

elmwood memorial hospital

1411 first street

tucson, az 85062

Name _____   Date _____

E. Write a sentence to show each use of capital letters.

1. Name of a holiday _____
_____

2. Name of a restaurant in your community _____
_____

3. Name of a favorite book _____
_____

4. Name of an author _____
_____

5. Name of a business firm in or near your community _____
_____

6. Name of a country _____
_____

7. Name of a song _____
_____

8. Name of a magazine _____
_____

9. A direct quotation _____
_____

10. Name of a musician _____
_____

11. A title that is written as part of a name _____
_____

12. Name of a college or university _____
_____

13. Name of a river or lake _____
_____

14. Name of an actor or actress _____
_____

Using End Punctuation

> - Use a **period** at the end of a declarative sentence.
>   EXAMPLE: Sunlight is essential for the growth of plants.
> - Use a **question mark** at the end of an interrogative sentence.
>   EXAMPLE: How much sunlight does a plant need?

A. Use a period or question mark to end each sentence below.

1. Doesn't Sandra's family now live in Missouri____

2. "Snow Time" is a well-known poem____

3. Isn't someone knocking at the door, Beth____

4. Didn't Janice ask us to meet her at 2:30 this afternoon____

5. In Yellowstone Park, we saw Morning Glory Pool, Handkerchief Pool, and Old Faithful____

6. The greatest library in ancient times was in Alexandria, Egypt____

7. Aren't the employees' checks deposited in a different bank____

8. Will Ms. Wilson start interviewing applicants at 10:00 A.M.____

9. My uncle has moved to Calgary, Alberta____

10. Corn, oats, and soybeans are grown in Iowa____

11. Isn't Alex the chairperson of our committee____

12. I've mowed the lawn, pulled the weeds, and raked the leaves____

13. Did the American Revolution begin on April 19, 1775____

14. Is El Salvador in Central America____

B. Add the correct end punctuation where needed in the paragraphs below.

Did you know that experts say dogs have been around for thousands of years____ In fact, they were the first animals to be made domestic____ The ancestors of dogs were hunters____ Wolves are related to domestic dogs____ Like wolves, dogs are social animals and prefer to travel in groups____ This is called pack behavior____

There have been many famous dogs throughout history____ Can you name any of them____ In the eleventh century, one dog, Saur, was named king of Norway____ The actual king was angry because his people had removed him from the throne, so he decided to make them subjects of the dog____ The first dog in space was a Russian dog named Laika____ Laika was aboard for the 1957 journey of *Sputnik*____ Most people have heard of Rin Tin Tin and Lassie____ These dogs became famous in movies and television____

There are several hundred breeds of dogs throughout the world____ The smallest is the Chihuahua____ A Chihuahua weighs less than two pounds____ Can you think of the largest____ A Saint Bernard or a Mastiff can weigh over 150 pounds____

> ■ Use a **period** at the end of an imperative sentence.
>   EXAMPLE: Open this jar of tomatoes for me, please.
> ■ Use an **exclamation point** at the end of an exclamatory sentence and after an interjection that shows strong feelings. If a command expresses great excitement, use an exclamation point at the end of the sentence.
>   EXAMPLES: Look at the stars! Ouch! I'm so excited!

C. Add periods or exclamation points where needed in these sentences below.

1. Answer the telephone, Michael____

2. Please clean the kitchen for me____

3. Oh____ I can't believe how late it is____

4. Hurry____ The plane is leaving in a few minutes____

5. Carry the bags to the check-in counter____

6. Then run to the waiting area____

7. Hold that seat for me____

8. I can't miss the flight____

9. Stop____ Stop____ You forgot your ticket____

10. Please slow down____

11. Sit down, and put on your seat belt____

12. We're off____

13. Look how small the city is____

14. Please put on your seat belt____

15. Obey the captain's orders____

16. I can't wait until we land____

17. Please give me that magazine____

18. Look____ We're about to land____

D. Add the correct end punctuation where needed in the paragraphs below.

Mr. Henry Modine lives in San Francisco, California____ He often exclaims, "What a wonderful town____" What do you think he does for a living____ Mr. Modine owns a fishing boat, *The Marlin*____ In all of San Francisco, there are few boats as fine as *The Marlin*____ Henry Modine named his boat after the fish his customers like the best – the marlin____ Henry guarantees his customers a fish if they come out on his boat____

"Fantastic____" shouts Henry when someone hooks a marlin____ Henry then says "Bring it in____" Part of Henry's job is to help the fishers reel in the big fish____ Can you believe that some marlins weigh 1,000 pounds or more____ Most of the ones Henry's customers catch weigh about 100 pounds____ They are either striped marlins or black marlins____

Using Commas

> - Use a **comma** between words or groups of words that are in a series.
>   EXAMPLE: Pears, peaches, plums, and figs grow in the southern states.
> - Use a comma before a conjunction in a compound sentence.
>   EXAMPLE: The farmers planted many crops, and they will work long hours to harvest them.
> - Use a comma after a subordinate clause when it begins a sentence.
>   EXAMPLE: After we ate dinner, we went to a movie.

A. Add commas where needed in the sentences below.

1. Frank Mary and Patricia are planning a surprise party for their parents.

2. It is their parents' fiftieth wedding anniversary and the children want it to be special.

3. They have invited the people their father used to work with their mother's garden club members and long-time friends of the family.

4. Even though the children are grown and living in their own homes it will be hard to make it a surprise.

5. Mr. and Mrs. Slaughter are active friendly and involved in many things.

6. For the surprise to work everyone will have to be sure not to say anything about their plans for that day.

7. This will be especially hard for the Knudsens but they will do their best.

8. Since every Sunday the families have dinner together the Knudsens will have to become very good actors the week of the party.

> - Use a comma to set off a quotation from the rest of a sentence.
>   EXAMPLES: "I want to go with you," said Paul.
>   Paul said, "I want to go with you."

B. Add commas before or after the quotations below.

1. "We're sorry that we have to cancel our plans" said Earl.

2. Carmen said "But we've done this every week for ten years!"

3. Jeanette said "We have to leave town."

4. Ivan asked "Can't you put it off just one day?"

5. "No I'm afraid we can't" said Earl.

6. "Then we'll just start over the following week" said Carmen cheerfully.

7. Jeanette said "I bet no one else has done this."

8. "I sure hate to spoil our record" said Earl.

9. "Don't worry about it" said Ivan.

10. "Yes everything will work out" said Jeanette.

> - Use a comma to set off the name of a person who is being addressed.
>   EXAMPLE: Emily, are you ready to go?
> - Use a comma to set off words like yes, no, well, and oh at the beginning of a sentence.
>   EXAMPLE: Yes, as soon as I find my jacket.
> - Use a comma to set off an appositive.
>   EXAMPLE: Felix, Emily's dog, is entered in a dog show.

C. Add commas where needed in the sentences below.

1. Anthony a grocery store owner was planning for a busy day.

2. "Diane would you open the store at 9 o'clock?" said Anthony.

3. "Of course that's the time we always open," said Diane.

4. "Pierre the chef at Elaine's will be coming by," he said.

5. Kelly said "Stephanie I'd like some fresh peanuts."

6. "Yes but how many pounds would you like?" answered Stephanie.

7. Ms. Harmon asked "Martin what kind of fresh fruit do you have?"

8. "Well let me check what came in this afternoon," said Martin.

9. Alan the butcher had to wait on fifteen customers.

10. "I don't have time to wait Alan," said Carol.

11. The manager Juan told everyone to be patient.

12. "Please it will go quickly if you all take a number," said Juan.

13. "Yes you're right as usual," said the crowd.

14. Martin the produce manager went behind the counter to help.

15. Well they had sold all of their grapes and tomatoes before noon.

16. "We only have one bushel of green beans left" said Martin.

17. Mr. Loster bought cherries bananas and corn.

18. He was planning a special dinner for Sara his wife.

19. Mr. Loster spent the afternoon cooking baking and cleaning.

20. Today July 18 was her birthday.

D. Add commas where needed in the paragraph below.

Men women boys and girls from across the nation participate in the Special Olympics. Because of this event patterned after the Olympic games boys and girls with disabilities have opportunities to compete in a variety of sports. The Special Olympics includes competition in track swimming and gymnastics. Volunteers plan carefully and they work hard to insure that the event will be challenging rewarding and worthwhile for all the participants. One of my neighbors Chris Bell once worked as a volunteer. "It was an experience that I'll never forget" he said.

Using Quotation Marks and Apostrophes

- Use **quotation marks** to show the exact words of a speaker. Use a comma or another punctuation mark to separate the quotation from the rest of the sentence. A quotation may be placed at the beginning or at the end of a sentence. Begin the quote with a capital letter.
  EXAMPLES: Pat said, "Please take the dog for a walk." "Please take the dog for a walk," said Pat.
- A quotation may also be divided within the sentence.
  EXAMPLE: "Pat," said Scott, "I just returned from a walk!"

A. Add quotation marks and commas where needed in the sentences below.

1. Wait for me said Laura because I want to go with you.

2. Kim, did you write an article about spacecraft? asked Tom.

3. Where is the manager's desk? inquired the stranger.

4. Joanne asked What is Eric's address?

5. David asked How long did Queen Victoria rule the British Empire?

6. Carlos, did you bring your interesting article? asked the teacher.

7. Good morning said Cindy.

8. Doug asked Did Jim hurt himself when he fell?

9. The meeting begins in ten minutes said Rico.

10. Hoan, you're early said Melissa.

11. Come on, said the coach you'll have to play harder to win this game!

12. Tony said, I know you'll do well in your new job. You're a hard worker.

- Use an **apostrophe** in a contraction to show where a letter or letters have been taken out.
  EXAMPLES: I **can't** remember your name. **I'll** have to think about it.
- Use an apostrophe to form a possessive noun. Add -'s to most singular nouns. Add -' to most plural nouns. Add -'s to a few nouns that have irregular plurals.
  EXAMPLES: **Dina's** house is made of brick. All the **neighbors'** houses are wooden. The **children's** treehouse is wooden.

B. Write the words in which an apostrophe has been left out. Insert apostrophes where they are needed.

1. Kate, didnt you want Sues job? _____

2. Havent you seen Pauls apartment? _____

3. Jim didnt hurt himself when he fell off Toms ladder. _____

4. The employees paychecks didnt arrive on time. _____

Using Colons and Hyphens

> - Use a **colon** after the greeting in a business letter.
>   EXAMPLES: Dear Mr. Johnson: Dear Sirs:
> - Use a colon between the hour and the minute when writing the time.
>   EXAMPLES: 1:30   6:15   11:47
> - Use a colon to introduce a list.
>   EXAMPLE: Our grocery list included the following items: chicken, milk, eggs, and broccoli.

A. Add colons where needed in the sentences below.

1. At 2 1 0 this afternoon, the meeting will start.

2. Please bring the following materials with you pencils, paper, erasers, and a notebook.

3. The meeting should be over by 4 3 0.

4. Those of you on the special committee should bring the following items cups, paper plates, forks, spoons, and napkins.

5. The meeting will deal with the following pool hours, swimming rules, and practice schedules.

6. The lifeguards will meet this evening from 8 0 0 to 1 0 0 0 to discuss responsibilities.

7. We will read the letter at 3 0 0 and have a question-and-answer session.

> - Use a **hyphen** between the parts of some compound words.
>   EXAMPLES: twenty-one   sister-in-law   go-getter   well-behaved
>   air-conditioned middle-aged   sixty-six   great-grandfather
>   blue-green   old-fashioned second-story ninety-two
> - Use a hyphen to separate the syllables of a word that is carried over from one line to the next.
>   EXAMPLE: When the coach has finished his speech, the class members will be allowed to use the pool.

B. Add hyphens where needed in the sentences below.

1. We decided to attend a class on how to use less water when garden ing.

2. Our lawn and old fashioned flower gardens need too much water.

3. The sign up sheet at the door was for those who wanted to be on a mailing list.

4. Twenty seven people had already signed up.

5. We saw that our son and daughter in law were there, too.

6. Hank spotted them sitting on an aisle near the center of the audi torium.

7. The speaker was a well known expert on gardening.

8. We sat next to our family and learned about long term plans for water conservation.

Unit 4 Test

In which sentences is a capital letter needed?

1. **A** ○ Have you read *Nature's way*?
   B ○ Spanish is his native language.
   C ○ The judge ran for re-election.
   D ○ Their anniversary is in May.

2. **A** ○ Jesse lost the directions.
   B ○ His favorite sandwich is italian meatball.
   C ○ I called for a doctor's appointment.
   D ○ The television station went off the air.

3. **A** ○ Please leave me alone.
   B ○ The children remained calm.
   C ○ It got cold early this fall.
   D ○ where is the cheese I just bought?

4. **A** ○ February 25, 1998
   B ○ Dear friend,
   C ○ Toronto, ontario
   D ○ Yours truly,

5. **A** ○ "The Sound of Silence"
   B ○ "Alan," said Teresa, "don't move."
   C ○ Frank said, "see me after work."
   D ○ "No, I don't," replied Anna.

6. **A** ○ My birthday is in June.
   B ○ Turn off the radio.
   C ○ He read from *The News Dispatch*.
   D ○ Sharon prefers doctor Ogata.

Which sentences are capitalized correctly?

7. **A** ○ Do you know Dr. Gonzalez, janet?
   B ○ The german tourists were friendly.
   C ○ Pat said, "please come soon."
   D ○ He met Mayor Winston today.

8. **A** ○ My dear barbara,
   B ○ Sincerely Yours,
   C ○ Fairmont, VA 30097
   D ○ 322 w. Laroche St.

In which sentences is end punctuation used correctly?

9. **A** ○ I've never had such a great time?
   B ○ Did you know there's a blizzard outside.
   C ○ I came by to see how you are feeling!
   D ○ I don't know where my sock is.

10. **A** ○ Please don't go alone.
    B ○ Why are you here!
    C ○ Can you imagine what happened.
    D ○ Did he say anything else!

In which sentences is the colon used correctly?

11. **A** ○ Will you be done: by 100?
    B ○ I woke up at: 730.
    C ○ Bring these: items socks, shoes, and food.
    D ○ Before 4:30, it was bright and sunny.

12. **A** ○ Dear Ms. Phelps:
    B ○ My Dear Aunt:
    C ○ Yours truly:
    D ○ 635: P.M.

In which sentences is the hyphen used correctly?

13. **A** ○ I saw a beautiful-blue green fish.
    B ○ Dan and Christine have always cele-brated their birthdays together.
    C ○ My grandmother is ninety two-years old.

14. **A** ○ The second story-window is broken, and it needs to be fixed soon.
    B ○ My sister in-law lives in Toronto, Ontario.
    C ○ Her new puppy is well-behaved.

Name _____   **Date** _____

In which sentences are commas used correctly?

15.
A ○ "I can't go today, Sam" Tony said.

B ○ After fishing we ate, swam and relaxed.

C ○ Charles wants to go but, Tom can't.

D ○ Dan, my neighbor, said he will meet us.

16.
A ○ Oh I know I can do it, if I try.

B ○ Jim told us "Be careful, not to slip!"

C ○ Did you use sugar, cinnamon, and nutmeg?

D ○ I called but, you weren't home.

17.
A ○ James can you go, or not?

B ○ Once he learns, Kevin will teach me to ski.

C ○ Well I guess I'll go, now.

D ○ My oldest friend Andrew, moved to Houston.

18.
A ○ Karen asked, "How can you tell?"

B ○ First I measured and then, I cut.

C ○ How old are, you Maria?

D ○ Since it rained we wrote letters, and read.

19.
A ○ Yes, it's a good thing, we found out.

B ○ "No" said Juan, "I don't want any."

C ○ He lives in New Orleans, Louisiana.

D ○ Who is the one, who did this?

20.
A ○ Men, women and children are invited.

B ○ A good neighbor's, Ted Barnes, house was flooded.

C ○ Michael asked "What happened here?"

D ○ We went first, and they followed shortly after.

In which sentences are quotation marks used incorrectly?

21.
A ○ "When," asked Joseph, "are you leaving?"

B ○ Sara told Scott, "I passed the test!"

C ○ "Tell me when to stop," said Mary.

D ○ "Gunnar added, I would never do that!"

22.
A ○ "I can't believe the time! exclaimed Bert.

B ○ Paul asked, "Where are you going to dinner?"

C ○ "Now," said Stephanie, "we can relax."

D ○ "I'm going to sit outside and read," said Sara.

23.
A ○ "Wait for me!" cried Jake.

B ○ Tim said, "I can see for miles."

C ○ "Well, said Ellen, it's not what I had imagined."

D ○ "Do you think it will storm?" asked Holly.

24.
A ○ "Don't worry," said Manuel. Everything is fine."

B ○ "Let me tell you what I saw," said Joe.

C ○ Laura asked, "What time should we meet?"

D ○ "Brett," said Louis, "bring in the lawn chairs."

25.
A ○ Roger said, "Nobody ever does what I ask."

B ○ My friend, said Ross, "it's been a good year."

C ○ "Let's look at houses," said Jalia.

D ○ "Wait until you see the view!" said Todd.

26.
A ○ "Show me which way they went," said Michelle.

B ○ "Since you left," said Bill, "things are not the same."

C ○ Beth said, "I voted for Judge Jackson."

D ○ "Doug said, He didn't want to go to Minneapolis, Minnesota."

Choose the sentences that need apostrophes.

27.
A ○ Our dogs fur is thicker in winter.

B ○ Your gloves are in the car.

C ○ Our neighbors bought a dog.

D ○ Keith brought home two loaves of bread.

28.
A ○ The copies she made were difficult to read.

B ○ Club members must volunteer ten hours a week.

C ○ The childrens poems were the hit of the talent show.

D ○ Two rooms must be reserved for the party.

Writing Sentences

> - Every sentence has a base consisting of a simple subject and a simple predicate.
>   EXAMPLE: Amanda baked.
> - Expand the meaning of a sentence by adding adjectives, adverbs, and prepositional phrases to the sentence base.
>   EXAMPLE: **My cousin** Amanda baked **a delicious orange cake for dessert.**

A. Expand the meaning of each sentence base by adding adjectives, adverbs, and/or prepositional phrases. Write each expanded sentence below.

1. (Carl swam.)

_____

2. (Clock ticked.)

_____

3. (Snow falls.)

_____

4. (Sun rose.)

_____

5. (Fireworks exploded.)

_____

B. Imagine two different scenes for each sentence base below. Write an expanded sentence to describe each scene you imagine.

1. (Students listened.) **a.** _____

   b. _____

2. (Jason wrote.) **a.** _____

   b. _____

3. (Kamal played.) **a.** _____

   b. _____

4. (Juan drove.) **a.** _____

   b. _____

5. (We helped.) **a.** _____

   b. _____

Writing Topic Sentences

> ■ A **topic sentence** states the main idea of a paragraph. It is often placed at the beginning of a paragraph.
> EXAMPLE:
> **Mario was asked to write an article about the new recreation center for the school paper.** He wrote a list of questions to ask. He interviewed the park superintendent. He found out about the old park and why it was necessary to build a recreation center.

A. Underline the topic sentence in each paragraph below.

1. Mario knew that having good questions was very important to a successful interview. He thought carefully about what he wanted to know. Then he divided his questions into groups. Some were about the building. Some were about recreation. Others were about the staff.

2. He wanted to include something about the history of the park. He found out who first owned the land. He also asked how people had used the park over the years.

3. Mario found out that the park was nearly as old as the town itself. It had been the scene of picnics, baseball games, carnivals, concerts, and holiday festivals. Political meetings had also been held there.

B. Write a topic sentence for each group of sentences below.

1. Topic Sentence: _____
   a. James Leland was the park superintendent.
   b. He had worked in the field of recreation and sports all his adult life.
   c. His father had been a high school teacher and coach.
   d. His grandfather had been a popular baseball player.

2. Topic Sentence: _____
   a. Mario enjoyed talking to James.
   b. He found out more than he had ever expected.
   c. James told him why the community needed the center.
   d. The city had grown, and it needed to provide recreation for its residents.

C. Think of a topic you are interested in. Write the topic on the line. Then write a topic sentence.

Topic: _____

Topic Sentence: _____

_____

Writing Supporting Details

- The idea expressed in the topic sentence can be developed with sentences containing **supporting details.** Details can include facts, examples, and reasons.

A. Circle the topic sentence, and underline only the sentences containing supporting details in the paragraph below.

Mario asked Theresa to help him with the article. She would write out the tape-recorded interviews. She would also make suggestions for changes. Theresa is very athletic. Finally, they would both work on typing the article.

B. After each topic sentence, write five sentences containing supporting details.

1. You must be organized when writing an article.

   a. _____

   b. _____

   c. _____

   d. _____

   e. _____

2. It is important to learn all you can about your topic.

   a. _____

   b. _____

   c. _____

   d. _____

   e. _____

C. Write four sentences that contain supporting details for the topic sentence you wrote in Exercise C, page 96.

Topic Sentence: _____

   a. _____

   b. _____

   c. _____

   d. _____

Ordering Information Within a Paragraph

- One way to organize information in a paragraph is to put it in **chronological order**—the time in which events occurred. Words such as first, next, second, then, finally, and later are used to indicate the order in which events happen. EXAMPLE: **First,** Mario checked his tape recorder. **Then** he left for the interview.
- Another way to organize information is to use **spatial order.** Words such as above, near, over, beside, right, left, closer, farther, up, and down are used to express spatial relationships. EXAMPLE: The bald eagle sat on **top** of the tree. He watched the pond **below.**

A. Read each paragraph below and tell whether it is in chronological order or spatial order. For the paragraph in chronological order, underline the time order words. For the paragraph in spatial order, underline the words that indicate spatial order.

1.   The park board of directors must first approve the architect's design for the

recreation center. Then they must develop and approve a budget for the construction

of the center. Finally, they can give approval to construction of the center.

Order: _____

2.   The plan for the recreation center includes play areas for young children. A slide

and swingset will be built next to a large sand box. A jungle gym will be to the left

of the slide. Children will be able to climb to the top of the jungle gym and then

jump down to the ground.

Order: _____

B. Number the details below in chronological order.

_____ Then early in March, the park board of directors approved the architect's design.

_____ Next, the budget was approved in April.

_____ The center's roof was finally completed in August.

_____ In January, the architect first finished his design.

C. Choose one of the scenes below. Write a paragraph of at least four sentences describing the scene. Use spatial order words to show location.

Scenes: your house, a ballpark, a restaurant, a theater, a friend's house

_____

_____

_____

_____

Topic and Audience

> ■ The **topic** of a story or an article is the subject written about.
> ■ The **audience** is the group of readers.
>   EXAMPLES: students, family members, neighbors, readers of a newspaper

A. Choose the most likely audience for each topic listed below.

a. first-graders   **b.** the city council   **c.** high-school students   **d.** parents

_____ 1. Star Athlete Visits Students at Recreation Center

_____ 2. Study Shows Connection between Time Spent Exercising and Student Progress in School

_____ 3. Peter Rabbit Here for Hop and Jump Exercises

_____ 4. Council Considers Tax Plans to Finance Recreation Center

_____ 5. Tryouts for High School Track Team on Friday

_____ 6. Study Shows City Budget Shortfall Next Year

_____ 7. Kelsey School Parents' Night Next Thursday

_____ 8. Officer Safety to Visit Young Students Next Week

_____ 9. State University Considers Raising Tuition

_____ 10. Governor Approves Funds to Expand City Bus Service

B. Read the paragraph below. Then answer the questions that follow.

On Tuesday evening, May 2, 1994, at 6:00, Hawkeye, the mascot of the Child Protection Foundation, will be at the park with his handler, Officer Roy Meyers. While Hawkeye, the long-eared hound, entertains the youngsters, Officer Meyers will discuss the topic "Keeping Your Children Safe." This unusual pair has traveled across the state to introduce the findings on topics such as accidents in the home, hazardous toys, and bike safety.

1. What is the topic of the paragraph?

   _____

2. Name two possible audiences for the paragraph.

   _____

3. Explain why each audience might be interested.

   Audience 1: _____

   Audience 2: _____

C. Choose a topic in which you are interested. Write the name of the topic, and name the audience it would be most likely to interest.

   Topic: _____

   Audience: _____

Clustering

> ■ A **clustering diagram** shows how ideas relate to a particular topic. The topic is written in the center. Related ideas are written around the topic. Lines show the connections between the ideas.
>
> EXAMPLE:
>
> establishment — park — political meetings
> holidays — carnivals
> picnics
>
> **Topic Sentence:** The recreation center will be built on land that was once a park.

A. Read each paragraph below. Notice the underlined topic sentence as you read. Then fill in each cluster to show how the details relating to that topic sentence could have been chosen.

1. <u>Mario had a great deal of work to do for the article.</u> He had to finish the interviews, decide what information to use, and write a rough draft. He then had to revise the draft, type the final copy, and proofread it.

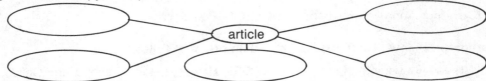

article

2. <u>Theresa worked hard on the article.</u> She typed the interviews. She edited the article. She organized the rough draft. Finally, she helped with the final revision and proofreading.

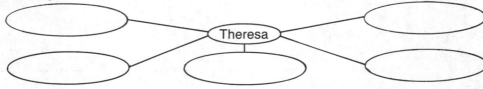

Theresa

B. Rewrite the topic sentence you wrote on page 97, Exercise C.

Topic Sentence: _____

C. Write that topic from Exercise B in the center of the cluster below. Then fill in the cluster with details that would support your main topic.

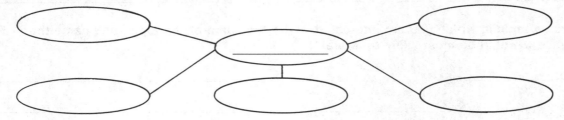

Outlining

- Before you write about a topic, organize your thoughts by making an **outline.** An outline consists of the title of the topic, **main headings** for the main ideas, and **subheadings** for supporting ideas.
- Main headings are listed after Roman numerals. Subheadings are listed after capital letters.

Topic: The need for a recreation center

I. Problems with park
   A. Age of equipment
   B. Limited usefulness for residents
II. Advantages of recreation center
   A. Wide range of uses
   B. Safe, up-to-date equipment

- **Refer to your topic sentence on page 100, Exercise B. Write an outline based on the clusters, using the example outline as a guide.**

Topic: _____

  I. _____

    A. _____

    B. _____

 II. _____

    A. _____

    B. _____

III. _____

    A. _____

    B. _____

IV. _____

    A. _____

    B. _____

 V. _____

    A. _____

    B. _____

Preparing Interview Questions

> ■ Writers use interviews to get information. Good interview questions will
> encourage the person being interviewed to talk freely about the subject.
> EXAMPLES: Why do we need a recreation center? Who will be involved
> in making decisions?
> ■ Avoid questions that can be answered either <u>yes</u> or <u>no</u> by beginning
> them with words such as <u>who</u>, <u>what</u>, <u>why</u>, and <u>how</u>.
> EXAMPLE: Why do we need a recreation center?

A. Write <u>who</u>, <u>what</u>, <u>when</u>, <u>where</u>, <u>why</u>, or <u>how</u> to complete each question.

1. _____ will vote on the budget for the recreation center?

2. _____ will be the various uses of the center?

3. _____ will the center be paid for?

4. _____ will the center be located?

5. _____ do you think a recreation center is necessary?

6. _____ will the center be completed?

B. Rewrite the questions below so that they cannot be answered <u>yes</u> or <u>no</u>.

1. Does the park have an interesting history?

_____

2. Is the location of the park good?

_____

3. Does the council have plans to raise local taxes?

_____

4. Will the townspeople have a say on the new recreation center?

_____

**C. Choose a topic and write three questions about it. Remember to begin each question
with <u>who</u>, <u>what</u>, <u>when</u>, <u>where</u>, <u>how</u>, or <u>why</u>.**

Topic: _____

1. _____

2. _____

3. _____

Writing Based on an Interview

- Many factual articles are based on information gathered in an interview. The writer asks questions about the subject he or she wants to cover and then uses the information to write an article.

- **Read the notes from the interview. Then read the paragraph that Mario and Theresa wrote, and answer the questions that follow.**

Question 1: James, how do you feel about the proposed recreation center?

Answer: It is definitely needed. The park is too small for our growing city and needs massive repairs anyway. It will be good for the whole city to have a well-equipped recreation center.

Question 2: Your family has been involved in sports for many years. How do you feel about the modern approach to physical fitness for people of all ages?

Answer: Physical fitness is vital for everyone. That's why the new recreation center is so important. It will offer facilities and programs for everyone, regardless of age or current fitness levels.

Question 3: What will the recreation center include?

Answer: The center will house an indoor pool, a small ice rink, two gyms, meeting rooms, arts-and-crafts facilities, and locker rooms with showers. We also hope to include a weight-lifting room.

> According to Mr. James Leland, park superintendent, the new recreation center will be a welcome addition to the city's facilities. The old park is now outdated and can no longer fill the needs of the people. Mr. Leland recommends that the park be the site of the new recreation center. Its facilities, which will include an indoor pool and two gyms, will fit everyone's needs, regardless of age or current fitness levels.

1. Does the author quote Mr. Leland exactly? _____

2. Write one sentence in the article that came from question 1.

   _____

   _____

3. Write one sentence in the article that came from question 3.

   _____

   _____

4. Write another question that Mario could have asked Mr. Leland.

   _____

5. What other things will the recreation center include that were not in the article?

   _____

Name _____ Date _____

Revising and Proofreading

- **Revising** gives you a chance to rethink and review what you have written and to improve your writing. Revise by adding words and information, by taking out unneeded words and information, and by moving words, sentences, and paragraphs around.
- **Proofreading** has to do with checking spelling, punctuation, grammar, and capitalization. Use proofreader's marks to show changes needed in your writing.

Proofreader's Marks

Take something out.

≡ Capitalize.   ⊙ Add a period.   ⑤ Correct spelling.

/ Make a small letter.   Add quotation marks.   ¶ Indent for new paragraph.

∧ Add a comma.   ∧ Add something.   Move something.

A. Rewrite the paragraph below. Correct the errors by following the proofreader's marks.

¶ The berryton city council today appruved plans today for construction of a New recreation center mayor june booth said the center to be located on the sight of the currant adams park will provide berryton residents with a variety of recreational programs" the center's facilities include will an indoor pool to gymnasiums, arts-and-crafts facilities, and a small ice rink and an indoor pool Several meating rooms will also be Included too for use buy various organizations.

_____

_____

_____

_____

_____

_____

_____

Name _____ Date _____

B. Read the paragraphs below. Use proofreader's marks to revise and proofread the paragraphs. Then write your revised paragraphs below.

Representatives from severals community organizations attended the meeting to express their support of the recreation center "Construction of this center is Long Overdue Are members will now have a central place in which to meat instead of crowding into each other's homes said Milton Sayre chairman of the berryton citizens senior league

plans call for a groundbreaking ceremony on thursday may 16 at 2 30 followed by a reception in adams park Construction is scheduled mayor booth supervisor john leland and city council members will participate all residents are invited to join them at the ceremoney

_____
_____
_____
_____
_____
_____
_____
_____
_____
_____
_____
_____
_____
_____
_____
_____

Unit 5, Composition
© Steck-Vaughn Publishing Company

Language Practice 7, SV 7163-5

Unit 5 Test

Read the paragraph. Then choose the correct answer to each question.

> Many Moroccans dress in very traditional clothing, wearing long robes and veils or turbans. Others wear modern Western clothing. Several languages are spoken in Morocco, including Arabic, Berber, French, and Spanish. Morocco's landscape is nearly as varied as the cultures that have influenced its people. You can find barren deserts, fertile farmlands, forested mountains, and sandy beaches all within this northwestern region of Africa.

1. Which sentence could best be used as a topic sentence for the paragraph above?

   A ○ Morocco's official language is Arabic.

   B ○ Morocco has many interesting sights and sounds.

   C ○ Many languages are spoken in Morocco.

   D ○ Morocco has a beautiful landscape.

2. Which sentence would add the most appropriate supporting detail to the paragraph above?

   A ○ My brother wants to go to Morocco.

   B ○ Spanish is also spoken in Mexico.

   C ○ A popular Moroccan dish is called *couscous*.

   D ○ You can see the French and Spanish influences in Moroccan art.

3. Which audience would be the most interested in this paragraph?

   A ○ football players   **B** ○ waitresses   **C** ○ preschool children   **D** ○ travelers

Choose the correct answer to each question.

4. Which word does not indicate chronological order?

   A ○ finally   **C** ○ around

   B ○ next   **D** ○ then

5. Which sentence would come first in chronological order?

   A ○ By February, the ground was frozen solid.

   B ○ The fall was uncommonly cold.

   C ○ At the end of the year, snow began piling up.

   D ○ Cold weather kept many travelers at home.

6. Which is not a way of organizing information or ideas?

   A ○ clustering   **C** ○ interviewing

   B ○ chronological order **D** ○ outlining

7. Which word indicates spatial order?

   A ○ nearly   **C** ○ region

   B ○ within   **D** ○ landscape

8. Which sentence does not use spatial order?

   A ○ The only phone booth is around the corne

   B ○ Go down the street a block, then turn left.

   C ○ You will find a telephone book inside the booth.

   D ○ Use it to look up the number of the statio

9. Which is not part of an outline?

   A ○ headings   **C** ○ audience

   B ○ title   **D** ○ subheadings

Choose the correct answer to each question.

10. Which is the best interview question?

    A ○ Will the city's orchestra do as well this year?

    B ○ Do you enjoy singing in front of a crowd?

    C ○ Are there any new goals for your company?

    D ○ Why did you decide to run for office?

11. Which word is not good for an interview question?

    A ○ how   **C** ○ does

    B ○ where   **D** ○ who

Read the outline below. Then answer the questions that follow.

Topic: Staying safe in your home
I. When you're at home
    A. Keep doors and windows locked
    B. Close shades or curtains at night
    C. _____
II. _____
    A. Leave lights on inside and outside
    B. Leave a radio on

12. Which fits best in subhead C?

    A ○ Don't answer the telephone

    B ○ Don't open the door to a stranger

    C ○ Don't watch television

    D ○ Don't leave your car outside

13. Which fits best in head II?

    A ○ When you're away from home

    B ○ Lighting your home

    C ○ Keeping people away

    D ○ How dogs guard homes

Which is the correct revision of each underlined sentence?

14. After the Pinskes Called mr. an Mrs. Fisk then for left the airport.

    A ○ The Pinskes called, after Dr. and Mrs. Fisk Then left for the airport.

    B ○ After the Pinskes calld. Mr. an Mrs. Fisk left for the airport.

    C ○ After the Pinskes called, Mr. and Mrs. Fisk left for the airport.

    D ○ The pinskes called and Dr. and Mrs. Fist left for the airport.

15. many peple visit wyoming not very many live there actually

    A ○ Although many people visit wyoming, not very many live there.

    B ○ Many people visit Wyoming but actually not very many live there.

    C ○ Although people visit Wyoming, actually not many people live there.

    D ○ Although many people visit Wyoming, not very many actually live there.

Which shows the correct proofreader's marks for the revised numbered sentence?

16. In order to work with our program, please complete the attached application.

    A ○ in order to to work with our Program please compleat the attached application.

    B ○ to work with our program, attach a completed aplication.

    C ○ In order work with the program, please attach a application.

    D ○ in order to work with our pogram please complete the applicaton.

Dictionary: Guide Words

- A **dictionary** is a reference book that contains definitions of words and other information about their history and use.
- **Entries** in a dictionary are listed in **alphabetical order**.
- **Guide words** appear at the top of each dictionary page. Guide words show the first and last entry on the page.
  - EXAMPLE: The word <u>lease</u> would appear on a dictionary page with the guide words <u>learn</u> / <u>lesson</u>. The word <u>lever</u> would not.

A. Put a check in front of each word that would be listed on a dictionary page with the given guide words.

1. fade / flat	2. image / inform	3. radio / reach
_____ faster	_____ information	_____ rail
_____ face	_____ impossible	_____ rabbit
_____ flavor	_____ insect	_____ ranch
_____ fetch	_____ incomplete	_____ real
_____ flatter	_____ ignore	_____ raw
_____ factory	_____ immense	_____ raccoon
_____ flag	_____ indeed	_____ raft
_____ fancy	_____ improve	_____ read
_____ flop	_____ insist	_____ ramp
_____ fertile	_____ infect	_____ rate
_____ flow	_____ imagine	_____ reduce
_____ flame	_____ inherit	_____ rake

B. Number the words in each column in the order of their appearance in a dictionary. Then write the words that could be the guide words for each column.

1. _____ / _____	2. _____ / _____	3. _____ / _____
_____ bedroom	_____ dine	_____ fire
_____ blend	_____ depend	_____ face
_____ blame	_____ determine	_____ free
_____ biography	_____ department	_____ finger
_____ block	_____ district	_____ faint
_____ blink	_____ disease	_____ flower
_____ bear	_____ disturb	_____ family
_____ benefit	_____ discard	_____ follow
_____ believe	_____ difference	_____ fair
_____ beach	_____ dessert	_____ flavor

Dictionary: Syllables

- A **syllable** is a part of a word that is pronounced at one time. Dictionary entry words are divided into syllables to show how they can be divided at the end of a writing line.
- A **hyphen** (-) is placed between syllables to separate them.
  EXAMPLE: quar-ter-back
- If a word has a beginning or ending syllable of only one letter, do not divide it at the end of a writing line so that one letter stands alone.
  EXAMPLES: a-fraid   bus-y

A. Find each word in a dictionary. Then write each word with a hyphen between each syllable.

1. allowance _____
2. porridge _____
3. harness _____
4. peddle _____
5. character _____
6. hickory _____
7. solution _____
8. variety _____
9. talent _____
10. weather _____

11. brilliant _____
12. enthusiasm _____
13. dramatic _____
14. employment _____
15. laboratory _____
16. judgment _____
17. kingdom _____
18. recognize _____
19. usual _____
20. yesterday _____

B. Write two ways in which each word may be divided at the end of a writing line.

1. victorious _____ vic-torious _____   _____ victori-ous _____
2. inferior _____   _____
3. quantity _____   _____
4. satisfactory _____   _____
5. security _____   _____
6. possession _____   _____
7. thermometer _____   _____
8. getaway _____   _____

Name _____ Date _____

Dictionary: Definitions and Parts of Speech

- A dictionary lists the **definitions** of each entry word. Many words have more than one definition. In this case, the most commonly used definition is given first. Sometimes a definition is followed by a sentence showing a use of the entry word.
- A dictionary also gives the **part of speech** for each entry word. An abbreviation (shown below) stands for each part of speech. Some words may be used as more than one part of speech.
  - EXAMPLE: **mess** (mes) *n.* **1.** an untidy, usually dirty, condition. -*v.* to make untidy and dirty.

- **Use the dictionary samples below to answer the questions.**

cage (kāj) *n.* a structure in which animals can be kept. *v.* to lock up or keep in a cage.
cos-tume (kos′ tōōm) *n.* **1.** an outfit worn in pretending to be someone else: *Karla's costume was the nicest one in the play.* **2.** a type of dress associated with a particular people, place or time. -*v.* to provide with a costume.

cot-ton (kot′ ən) *n.* **1.** soft fibers that grow in a cluster on seed pods of certain plants and are used to make cloth. **2.** the plant on which these fibers grow. **3.** thread made from cotton fibers. **4.** cloth woven of cotton. -*adj.* made of cotton: *The cotton dress might shrink in warm water.*

1. Which words can be used as either a noun or a verb? _____

2. Which word can be used as an adjective?

   _____

3. Which word has the most meanings?

   _____

n.	noun
pron.	pronoun
v.	verb
adj.	adjective
adv.	adverb
prep.	preposition

4. Which word can be used as a noun or as an adjective? _____

5. Write the most commonly used definition of <u>costume</u>. _____

6. Write a sentence in which you use <u>cage</u> as a verb. _____

7. Write a sentence using the first definition of <u>costume</u>. _____

8. Use the second definition of <u>cotton</u> in a sentence. _____

Dictionary: Word Origins

- An **etymology** tells of an entry word's origin and development. Many dictionary entries include an etymology.
- The etymology is usually enclosed in brackets [ ] after the definition of the entry word. The language from which the entry word came into English is listed first, followed by the language from which that word came, and so on. Often the symbol ≤ is used to save space and stands for the phrase "is derived from" or "comes from."
  EXAMPLE: **tu-lip** (tōo′ lip, tyōo′ lip) [Lat. *Tulipa* < Turk. *tülibend,* turban < Pers. *dulband.*] The word *tulip* came into English from the New Latin word *Tulipa,* which came from the Turkish word *tülibend,* which meant "turban." The word *tülibend* came from the Persian word *dulband.*

■ **Use the dictionary samples below to answer the questions.**

e-mo-tion (i mō′ shən) *n.* strong feeling. [Middle French *emouvoir* to stir up, from Latin *exmovēre* to move away, disturb from *ex + movēre* to move.]
gup-py (gup′ ē) *n.* a small, brightly-colored freshwater fish. [After R. J. L. Guppy (1836–1916), who introduced the fish to England.]
line (līn) *n.* a long, narrow mark as with pen or pencil. [A combination of Old French *ligne* string, cord and Old English *line* cord, rope.]

load (lōd) *n.* **1.** that which is put on a pack animal to carry. **2.** cargo put on a ship, plane, train, or truck. [Middle English *lod,* from Old English *lād* support, carrying.]
mar-a-thon (mar′ a thon′) *n.* a cross-country foot race. [After *Marathon,* Greece (so called because in 490 B.C. a messenger ran from Marathon to Athens to announce a victory over the Persians).]

1. Which word comes from the name of a person? _____

2. Which word originally meant "to move"? _____

3. Which languages are in the history of the word <u>line</u>? _____

4. Which word comes from both Middle English and Old English? _____

5. Which word comes from the name of a place? _____

6. Which words have more than one language in their histories? _____

7. What is the meaning of the Latin word <u>exmovēre</u>? _____

8. Why is the guppy named after R. J. L. Guppy? _____

9. What did the Middle English word <u>lod</u> come from? _____

10. Why do we call a long race a marathon? _____

_____

11. Which word comes from a word that meant "support or carrying"? _____

12. Which word comes from the word <u>ligne</u>? _____

13. Which words come from French? _____

Using Parts of a Book

- A **title page** lists the name of a book and its author.
- A **copyright page** tells who published the book, where it was published, and when it was published.
- A **table of contents** lists the chapter or unit titles and the page numbers on which they begin. It is at the front of a book.
- An **index** gives a detailed list of the topics in a book and the page numbers on which each topic is found. It is in the back of a book.

A. Answer the questions below.

1. Where should you look for the page number of a particular topic? _____

2. Where should you look to find out who wrote a book? _____

3. Where should you look to get a general idea of the contents of a book? _____

4. Where should you look to find out when a book was published? _____

5. Where should you look to find the name of the book? _____

6. Where should you look to find out who published a book? _____

B. Use the table of contents below to answer the questions.

Table of Contents

Who Are the Sioux?	4	War and Defeat	24
The Tribe and Its Ways	6	The Sioux Today	28
Buffalo!	10	Glossary	30
Appearance	14	Important Dates	31
Warriors	18	Books to Read	31
Religion and Beliefs	22	Index	32

1. What is this book about? _____

2. On what pages can you read about the tribe and its ways? _____

3. On what pages can you read about war and defeat? _____

4. On what pages can you read about appearance? _____

5. What can you read about on pages 10–13? _____

6. What can you read about on pages 28–29? _____

7. Does the book contain a glossary? _____

8. Where is the index located? _____

Name _____ Date _____

Using the Library

■ Books are arranged on library shelves according to **call numbers**. Each
book is assigned a number from 000 to 999, according to its subject matter.
The following are the main subject groups for call numbers.

000–099	Reference	500–599	Science and Mathematics
100–199	Philosophy	600–699	Technology
200–299	Religion	700–799	The Arts
300–399	Social Sciences	800–899	Literature
400–499	Languages	900–999	History and Geography

A. Write the call number group in which you would find each book.

1. *World Almanac and Book of Facts* _____

2. *Mathematics for Today* _____

3. *Global Warming: A World Problem* _____

4. *Philosophy Through the Ages* _____

5. *Spanish: A Romance Language* _____

6. *Technology Takes Over* _____

7. *Splitting the Atom* _____

8. *The Encyclopedia of Mammals* _____

9. *The Impressionist School of Painting* _____

10. *Children's Stories from Around the World* _____

11. *The Study of Forgotten Societies* _____

12. *The New Russia* _____

13. *The Religions of the World* _____

14. *The Reader's Guide* _____

15. *Dance in North America* _____

B. Write the titles of three of your favorite books. Write the call number range beside each title.

1. _____

2. _____

3. _____

Name _____   Date _____

Using the Card Catalog

- The **card catalog** contains information cards on every book in the library. Some libraries are now computerized and have no card catalogs, but the information in the computer is filed in the same manner as the information in the card catalog.
- Each book has three cards in the catalog. The cards are filed separately according to: 1. the author's last name, 2. the subject of the book, and 3. the title of the book.
- Most smaller libraries use the **Dewey Decimal System** to organize their books. Each book is assigned a **call number** from 000 to 999, according to its subject matter.

A. Refer to the sample catalog card to answer the questions about one book.

Subject Card

Call number ——— 363.73   Air Pollution ———————— Subject

Author ——————— Baines, John D.

Title ——————— Conserving the atmosphere: an introduction to the problems confronting the earth's atmosphere, and what can be done to stop its destruction Austin, Texas: ——— Place published

Publisher ——— Raintree/Steck-Vaughn © 1989 ——— Date published

Number of pages ——— 48 p. illus. ——— Illustrated

1. What is the title? _____

2. Who is the author? _____

3. Who published it? _____ When was it published? _____

4. What is the call number? _____ How many pages does it have? _____

5. What is the general subject? _____

6. Does it contain illustrations? _____

B. Write <u>author</u>, <u>title</u>, or <u>subject</u> to tell which card you would look for to locate the book or books.

1. books about mountain climbing   _____

2. *Life in the Chinese Countryside*   _____

3. a book of short stories by O. Henry   _____

4. a book by Jane Austen   _____

Using an Encyclopedia

- An **encyclopedia** is a reference book that contains articles on many different topics. The articles are arranged alphabetically in volumes. Each volume is marked to show which articles are inside.
- Guide words are used to show the first topic on each page.
- At the end of most articles there is a listing of **cross-references** to related topics for the reader to investigate.

A. Find the entry for <u>Knute Rockne</u> in an encyclopedia. Then answer the following questions.

1. What encyclopedia did you use? _____

2. When did Knute Rockne live? _____

3. Where was he born? _____

4. Where did he go to college? _____

5. For what is he best known? _____

B. Find the entry for <u>Redwood</u> in an encyclopedia. Then answer the following questions.

1. What encyclopedia did you use? _____

2. Where does the redwood tree grow? _____

3. By what other name is it known? _____

4. What is special about this tree? _____

5. How tall do most redwoods grow? _____

C. Find the entry in an encyclopedia for a person in whom you are interested. Then answer the following questions.

1. Who is your subject? _____

2. What encyclopedia did you use? _____

3. When did the person live? _____

4. Where did the person live? _____

5. What is it about the person that makes him or her famous? _____

_____

6. What cross-references are listed? _____

Using an Encyclopedia Index

> ■ Most encyclopedias have an **index** of subject titles, listed in alphabetical order. The index shows the volume and the page number where an article can be found. Some encyclopedias contain articles on many different topics. Other encyclopedias contain different articles relating to a broad general topic.

■ **Use the sample encyclopedia index to answer the questions below.**

Index

Acorn Squash, 1–6; 11–1759
   Baked, supreme, **1**–7
   Steamed, **1**–7
Appetizer(s), 1–841; *see also* Cocktail; Dip; Pickle and Relish; Spread
   Almonds, **1**–89
   Celery, stuffed, **1**–89
   Cheese Ball, **3**–429
Cabbage, 2–256; *see also* Salads, Coleslaw; Sauerkraut
   with bacon and cheese sauce, **1**–68
Flour, 5–705
   Peanut, **8**–1328
   Rice, **10**–1556
   Wheat, **12**–1935

1. In what volume would you find an article on stuffed celery? _____

2. On what page would you find information on cabbage with bacon and cheese sauce? _____

3. Are all articles on flour found in the same volume? _____

4. What are the cross-references for **Appetizers**? _____

5. Do the words in bold show the name of the volume or the name of the main food or ingredient? _____

6. Which main food or ingredient has articles in two volumes? _____

7. Information on which appetizers can be found in the same volume and on the same page? _____

_____

8. What main ingredient is found in Volume 5? _____

9. If you looked under **Dip**, what might you expect to find as a cross-reference? _____

_____

10. Information on what appetizer would be found in Volume 3? _____

11. Information on what ingredient is found on page 1328 in the encyclopedia? _____

Using Reference Sources

> ■ Use reference sources—dictionaries, encyclopedias, the *Readers' Guide to Periodical Literature,* thesauruses, atlases, and almanacs—to find information about people, places, or things with which you are not familiar. You can also use these sources to find out more about subjects that interest you.

A. Follow the directions below.

1. Choose a person from history that you would like to know more about.

   Person's name: _____

2. Name two reference sources that you can use to find information about this person.

   a. _____

   b. _____

3. Use one of the reference sources you named above. Find the entry for the person you are researching. Write the exact title of the reference.

   _____

4. Write a short summary of the information you found.

   _____

   _____

   _____

   _____

5. Name the source that would contain recent articles about this person.

   _____

6. Look up your person's name in the reference source you listed in number 5. Write the titles of three articles that were listed.

   a. _____

   b. _____

   c. _____

7. Which articles above, if any, can be found in your library?

   _____

8. Name a subject heading under which you might find more information on your person.

   _____

Name _____ Date _____

B. Follow the directions, and answer the questions.

1. Choose a country you would like to know more about.

   Name of country: _____

2. List four reference sources that you can use to find information about this country.

   a. _____   c. _____

   b. _____   d. _____

3. Find the entry for the country in one of the reference sources you listed.
   Write the exact title of the reference source.

   _____

4. Write a short summary of the information you found.

   _____

   _____

   _____

   _____

   _____

5. Find the entry for the country in one other reference source. Write the exact
   title of the reference source.

   _____

6. What new information did you find about the country?

   _____

   _____

   _____

C. Follow the directions, and answer the questions below.

1. In what state do you live? _____

2. Find the entry for your state in one of the reference sources. Write the exact

   title of the reference source. _____

3. Write a short summary of the information you found about your state.

   _____

   _____

   _____

   _____

Unit 6 Test

Refer to the dictionary samples to answer the questions that follow.

lem-on (lem′ ən) *n.* **1.** a small, oval citrus fruit with a yellow rind and sour pulp. **2.** a bright yellow color. *-adj.* **1.** being the color lemon. **2.** made from lemon: *I used lemon juice on the fish.* [Middle English *lymon,* from Middle French *limon.*]
load (lōd) *n.* **1.** something carried or to be carried in one trip. **2.** an amount that can be carried. **3.** something that is a burden.

-v. **1.** to place or put something. **2.** to supply abundantly. [Middle English *lode,* from Old English *lad,* a journey.]
lob-ster (läb′ ster) *n.* **1.** an edible, saltwater sea animal with five pairs of legs, one of which has pincer claws. **2.** the flesh of this animal used for food: *Do you like lobster?*

1. Which word has only one syllable?

   A ○ load **B** ○ lobster **C** ○ lemon

2. Which has the most definitions?

   A ○ load **B** ○ lobster **C** ○ lemon

3. Which word serves as only one part of speech?

   A ○ load **B** ○ lobster **C** ○ lemon

4. Which word is both a noun and an adjective?

   A ○ lobster **B** ○ load **C** ○ lemon

5. Which word originally meant "journey"?

   A ○ load **B** ○ lobster **C** ○ lemon

6. As which part of speech can load not be used?

   A ○ noun **B** ○ verb **C** ○ adjective

7. From how many other languages did lemon come?

   A ○ two **B** ○ three **C** ○ one

8. For which word is no etymology given?

   A ○ load **B** ○ lobster **C** ○ lemon

Tell which kind of catalog card you would refer to in order to find the book(s). Choose (A) for author card, (B) for subject card, or (C) for title card.

9. a novel by E. B. White   **A** ○ **B** ○ **C** ○

10. a book about Japan   **A** ○ **B** ○ **C** ○

11. *Wuthering Heights*   **A** ○ **B** ○ **C** ○

12. a play by William Shakespeare **A** ○ **B** ○ **C** ○

13. a book about animal behavior   **A** ○ **B** ○ **C** ○

Tell which reference source you would use to find the following information. Choose (A) for encyclopedia, (B) for thesaurus, (C) for *Readers' Guide,* or (D) for atlas.

14. an antonym for the word clever   **A** ○ **B** ○ **C** ○ **D** ○

15. information on Quebec, Canada   **A** ○ **B** ○ **C** ○ **D** ○

16. the location of the Saginaw River   **A** ○ **B** ○ **C** ○ **D** ○

17. a recent article on toxic waste   **A** ○ **B** ○ **C** ○ **D** ○

18. the life of Alexander the Great   **A** ○ **B** ○ **C** ○ **D** ○

19. an article written by George Maliff   **A** ○ **B** ○ **C** ○ **D** ○

20. a synonym for the word lovely   **A** ○ **B** ○ **C** ○ **D** ○

Choose the part of a book in which you would find the information.

21. the name of the author

    A ○ title page   **C** ○ table of contents

    B ○ copyright page   **D** ○ index

22. the page at the back of a book that lists where certain information can be found

    A ○ title page   **C** ○ table of contents

    B ○ copyright page   **D** ○ index

23. the date the book was published

    A ○ title page   **C** ○ table of contents

    B ○ copyright page   **D** ○ index

24. how many units are in the book

    A ○ title page   **C** ○ table of contents

    B ○ copyright page   **D** ○ index

Use the *Readers' Guide* samples to answer the questions.

HERTSGAARD, MARK
Onward and Upward with the Arts: Letting It Be.
il New Yorker 69: Jan 24, '94

KAGARLITSKY, BORIS
Make Them Truly Democratic.
The Nation 257:688–702 Dec '93

ICEBERGS
Icehunters. [International Ice Patrol; cover story] M. Dane. il map Popular Mechanics, 170:76–79 Oct '93

25. What article did Mark Hertsgaard write?

    A ○ Onward and Upward with the Arts

    B ○ Icehunters

    C ○ Make Them Truly Democratic

26. Which magazine has an article on icebergs?

    A ○ New Yorker

    B ○ Popular Mechanics

    C ○ The Nation

27. On which pages is the article by Boris Kagarlitsky?

    A ○ 688–702

    B ○ 170–176

    C ○ 76–79

28. Which article has a map?

    A ○ Onward and Upward with the Arts

    B ○ Make Them Truly Democratic

    C ○ Icehunters

Choose the correct answer for each question.

29. Which reference source does <u>not</u> use guide words?

    A ○ dictionary   **B** ○ atlas   **C** ○ encyclopedia

30. Which would you <u>not</u> use a dictionary to find?

    A ○ word origin   **B** ○ magazine articles   **C** ○ syllable

31. Which would you <u>not</u> find in a book?

    A ○ copyright page   **B** ○ table of contents   **C** ○ cross reference

Answer Key

Assessment Test (Pages 8–11)
A. 1. H **2.** A **3.** S **4.** S **B.** lock **C. 1.** C **2.** P **3.** S **4.** P **D. 1.** they will **2.** we have **E.** unhappy **F.** 2 **G.** The words in bold should be circled. **1.** IM; (You), **wait 2.** IN; you, **do believe 3.** E; I, **burned 4.** D; article, **made H. 1.** CP **2.** CS **I. 1.** I **2.** RO **3.** CS **J.** The word in bold should be labeled DO. [Before I left], I ate a good **breakfast**.
K. Common nouns: citizens, city, position; Proper nouns: Mayor Dumonte, Ms. Lopez **L.** The word in bold should be circled. nurse, **Ms. Abram, M. 1.** future **2.** past **N. 1.** are, were **2.** saw, knew **3.** begun, went **4.** threw, broke **O.** 2 **P.** The words in bold should be circled. **1.** IP, **Somebody 2.** OP, **her 3.** PP, **their 4.** SP, **We Q.** The word in bold should be circled. **jets**, their **R. 1.** adjective **2.** adverb **3.** adverb **4.** adjective **S.** The words in bold should be circled. on the bus, at me while

T. 956 E. Garden Circle
Bowman, TX 78787
April 13, 19___

Dear Steve,
  We're so excited you're coming to visit! Even little Scott managed to say, "Uncle Steve visit," which was pretty good for a child of only twenty–two months, wouldn't you agree? Oh, I want to be sure I have the information correct. Please let me know as soon as possible if any of this is wrong: flight 561 arrives at 3:10 P.M. on May 22. See you then.

Your sister,
Amanda

U. 1. 3 **2.** 1 **3.** 4 **4.** 2 **V.** 2 **W.** Although the decision to close Mayfield Park was unpopular, it proved to be the correct choice.
X. 1. adjective **2.** before **3.** Middle English **4.** jol-ly **Y. 1.** *Readers' Guide* **2.** card catalog **3.** atlas **4.** dictionary **5.** encyclopedia **Z. 1.** the Cree **2.** southwest into buffalo country **3.** Native Americans

Unit 1: Vocabulary
Synonyms and Antonyms (P. 13)
A.–D. Answers will vary.
Homonyms (P. 14)
A. 1. two, past **2.** too, to **3.** hear **4.** heard **5.** not, know, not **6.** seem, our **7.** won, medal **8.** weigh **9.** air, so, need **10.** rows **11.** knew, new, feet **12.** beet **13.** not, scene **14.** waist **B. 1.** piece **2.** alter **3.** too or two **4.** weigh or whey **5.** beach **6.** plane **7.** course **8.** seam **9.** new **10.** sail **11.** so **12.** brake **13.** weak **14.** rain or reign **15.** bear **16.** seen **17.** might **18.** hole **19.** horse **20.** forth **21.** night **22.** him **23.** threw **24.** groan **25.** rap **26.** pray **27.** straight **28.** soul **29.** here **30.** where, wear
Homographs (P. 15)
A. 1. b **2.** b **3.** a **4.** b **B. 1.** checkers **2.** duck **3.** can **4.** alight **C. 1.** stall **2.** snap **3.** squash **4.** quack **5.** punch
Prefixes (P. 16) Words and meanings will vary.
Suffixes (P. 17) Words and meanings will vary.
Contractions (P. 18)
A. 1. didn't **2.** wasn't **3.** we're **4.** isn't **5.** who's **6.** hadn't **7.** I'll **8.** I'm **9.** It's **10.** don't **11.** they've **12.** wouldn't **13.** won't **14.** doesn't **15.** weren't **16.** there's **17.** couldn't **18.** I've **19.** she'll **20.** they're **B. 1.** They're; They are **2.** They'll; They will **3.** it's; it is **4.** Mary's; Mary is **5.** she'll; she will **6.** doesn't; does not; he's; he is **7.** He'd; He would **8.** would've; would have **9.** aren't; are not; Tom's; Tom is **10.** they've; they have
Compound Words (P. 19)
A. Students should list any twelve of the following words: airline, understand, airport, seaport, air-condition underground, sandpaper, undersea, doorknob, blackbird, underline, blackberry, doorway, seabird **B.** Answers will vary.
Connotation/Denotation (P. 20)
A. 1. N **2.** + **3.** N **4.** – **5.** N **6.** – **7.** N **8.** + **9.** – **10.** N **B. 1.** horrible **2.** exciting **3.** unpleasant **4.** old **5.** mature **6.** over-the-hill

Idioms (P. 21)
A. Meanings will vary. **1.** in hot water **2.** was beside herself **3.** put their heads together **4.** was all ears **5.** throw in the towel **B.** Definitions will vary. **1.** hit the road **2.** eat crow **3.** burn the midnight oil **4.** cut me down to size
Unit 1 TEST, Pages 22–23
1. B **2.** C **3.** A **4.** D **5.** C **6.** A **7.** D **8.** B **9.** C **10.** B **11.** A **12.** D **13.** B **14.** A **15.** C **16.** D **17.** B **18.** A **19.** C **20.** D **21.** B **22.** D **23.** B **24.** A **25.** C **26.** B **27.** A **28.** C **29.** B **30.** C **31.** D **32.** B **33.** A **34.** B **35.** A **36.** D

Unit 2: Sentences
Recognizing Sentences (P. 24)
S should precede the following sentences, and each should end with a period: 1, 3, 5, 7, 10, 13, 14, 16, 17, 22, 23, 25, 28, 29, 30.
Types of Sentences (Pages 25–26)
A. 1. D **2.** IM **3.** IN **4.** IM **5.** IN **6.** IN **7.** D **8.** IN **9.** IM **10.** E **11.** IM **12.** IN **13.** IN **14.** D **15.** IN **16.** IM **17.** IN **18.** IM **19.** IN **20.** IM or E **21.** D **22.** IN **23.** IM **24.** E **25.** IN **26.** IM or E **27.** IM **28.** D **29.** IM **30.** E **31.** IM **32.** D **33.** IN **34.** IM **35.** IM **36.** D **37.** D **38.** IN **39.** E **40.** IN **41.** D **42.** D **43.** E **B.** Students should circle the following sentences: **1.** When will the train arrive? IN **2.** It is delayed by bad weather. D **3.** Juan and Shelly are on it. D **4.** I haven't seen them in two years! E **5.** They will stay with us for two weeks. D **6.** We have many things planned for them. D **7.** Sleep in the guest room. IM **8.** Juan used to work at a zoo. D **9.** Go in the reptile house. IM **10.** Each elephant had a name. D **11.** The elephants liked to train with Juan. D **12.** Sandra, the elephant, had a baby. D **13.** What did the zoo officials name the baby? IN **14.** They surprised Juan! E **15.** He never had an elephant named for him before! E
Complete Subjects and Predicates (Pages 27–28)
A. 1. Amy/built **2.** cleaner/will **3.** waltzes/were **4.** Victoria/ruled **5.** people/are **6.** visit/was **7.** rocket/was **8.** meeting/was **9.** farmers/are **10.** house/has **11.** heart/pumps **12.** computer/will **13.** friend/has **14.** silence/fell **15.** officers/were **16.** chef/prepared **17.** father/is **18.** Salazar/is **19.** Lightning/struck **20.** bicycling/are **21.** They/answered **22.** twilight/came **23.** Steve/has **24.** country/has **25.** We/will **26.** Butterflies/flew **27.** bus/was **B. and C.** Sentences will vary.
Simple Subjects and Predicates (P. 29)
A. 1. plants/sprouted **2.** program/was **3.** I/used **4.** truck/is **5.** beavers/created **6.** books/lined **7.** Hail/pounded **8.** I/bought **9.** subject/is **10.** bird/sang **11.** trunk/was **12.** sidewalk/had **B. 1.** vase/was **2.** children/had played. **3.** group/went **4.** He/drove **5.** skiers/were **6.** Birds/have **7.** Who/discovered **8.** I/am reading **9.** headlights/blinded **10.** page/is
Position of Subjects (P. 30)
1. The sunken treasure ship was where? **2.** Several sailboats were beyond the bridge. **3.** No one is in that room. **4.** The shouts of the victorious team came from the gymnasium. **5.** Beautiful flowers grew beside the walk. **6.** The surprise party is when? **7.** (You) Bring your sales report to the meeting. **8.** Only three floats were in the parade. **9.** The bark of the dog came from the yard. **10.** (You) Place the forks to the left of the plate.
Compound Subjects (P. 31)
A. Sentences 1, 3, 4, 6, 7, 8, 9, 10, 11, 13, 14, 15, 16, 18, 20, 21, and 22 have compound subjects. Sentences 2, 5, 12, 17, 19, 23, 24, and 25 have simple subjects. **1.** I/often **2.** Sandy/left **3.** I/will **4.** Delhi/are **5.** fire/spread **6.** Lenora/helped **7.** hiking/were **8.** Sydney/are **9.** I/had **10.** Mediterranean Sea/are **11.** Democrats/made **12.** The people/waved **13.** Jim/crated **14.** appearance/are **15.** dog/are **16.** Paul/are **17.** Tom/combed **18.** trees/bloom **19.** I/hummed **20.** antelope/once

21. Hiroshi/raked **22.** São Paulo/are **23.** gliding/is **24.** class/went **25.** doctor/asked **B.** Sentences will vary.

Compound Predicates (P. 32)

A. Sentences 1, 4, 6, 9, 10, 12, 13, 18, 19, 20, 22, and 23 have compound predicates. Sentences 2, 3, 5, 7, 8, 11, 14, 15, 16, 17, 21, 24, and 25 have simple predicates. **1.** Edward/grinned **2.** Plants/need **3.** kettles/were **4.** sister/buys **5.** Snow/covered **6.** Mr. Sanders/designs **7.** Popcorn/is **8.** Soccer/is **9.** ducks/quickly **10.** They/came **11.** Crystal/participated **12.** José/raked **13.** Perry/built **14.** We/collected **15.** Doug/arrived **16.** parents/are **17.** Garzas/live **18.** shingles/were **19.** audience/talked **20.** Automobiles/crowd **21.** apples/are **22.** group/grumbled **23.** She/worked **24.** Nelson Mandela/is **25.** supervisor/has **B.** Sentences will vary.

Combining Sentences (P. 33)

1. Lightning and thunder are part of a thunderstorm. **2.** Thunderstorms usually happen in the spring and bring heavy rains. **3.** Depending on how close or far away it is, thunder sounds like a sharp crack or rumbles. **4.** Lightning is very exciting to watch and can be very dangerous. **5.** Lightning causes many fires and harms many people. **6.** An open field or a golf course is an unsafe place to be during a thunderstorm. **7.** Benjamin Franklin wanted to protect people from lightning and invented the lightning rod. **8.** A lightning rod is a metal rod placed on the top of a building and connected to the ground by a cable.

Direct Objects (P. 34)

The words in bold should be labeled DO. **1.** can carry, **logs 2.** made, **rack 3.** Do, plan, **schedule 4.** won, **game. 5.** baked, **pie 6.** tuned, **piano 7.** take, **lessons 8.** composed, **melody 9.** enjoy, **stories 10.** orbited, **earth 11.** bought, **coat 12.** Did find, **glasses 13.** drove, **truck 14.** shrugged, **shoulders 15.** have finished, **work 16.** drink, **milk 17.** can solve, **problem 18.** made, **flag 19.** will learn, **something 20.** needs, **friends 21.** have found, **dime 22.** ate, **apple**

Indirect Objects (P. 35)

The words in bold should be labeled DO, and the words underlined twice should be labeled IO. **1.** give, Red Sea, **color 2.** gave, cashier, **check 3.** showed, audience, **tricks 4.** taught, them, **rules 5.** brought, us, **coins 6.** will give, reader, **pleasure 7.** Have written, brother, **letter 8.** made, us, **sandwiches 9.** gave, Mission Control, **data 10.** bought, friend, **etching 11.** did sell, Mike, **car 12.** have given, dog, **scrubbing 13.** Give, usher, **ticket 14.** brought, brother, **ring 15.** Hand, me, **pencil 16.** gave, orchestra, **break 17.** Show, me, **picture 18.** have given, you, **money 19.** Give, Lee, **message 20.** gave, town, **statue**

Independent and Subordinate Clauses (P. 36)

A. 1. Frank will be busy **2.** I have only one hour **3.** The project must be finished **4.** Gloria volunteered to do the typing **5.** The work is going too slowly **6.** I didn't think we could finish. **7.** What else should we do **8.** you can type it. **9.** we completed the project. **10.** We actually got it finished **B. 1.** who went shopping **2.** which is a mountain bike **3.** when the sale was over **4.** because she wanted some new things **5.** since he went late. **6.** where we went shopping **7.** who own the stores **8.** which is miles away **9.** because the bus was coming **10.** because we had run fast

Adjective Clauses (P. 37)

A. 1. that always points northward **2.** that measures earthquake tremors **3.** who work in science laboratories today **4.** that she has played in that position **5.** whose wrist was broken **6.** that I caught **7.** that contains a subordinate clause **8.** that I promised to show you **9.** that I read **B.** Sentences will vary.

Adverb Clauses (P. 38)

A. 1. when the cloudy skies cleared. **2.** Although the weather was mild and sunny **3.** after we arrived at the park **4.** because we were

prepared **5.** Since we had our jackets **6.** Although the clouds remained **7.** when we got to the top of the hill. **8.** After enjoying the beauty and the quiet for a while **9.** since it was still early. **10.** because we were so relaxed and happy. **B.** Sentences will vary.

Simple and Compound Sentences (P. 39)

A. Sentences 2, 3, 5, and 8 are simple sentences. Sentences 1, 4, 6, and 7 are compound sentences. **B. 1.** [You . . . rules,] or [you . . . race.] **2.** [I . . . test,] and [Maria . . . too.] **3.** [Shall . . . box,] or [do . . . here?] **4.** [We . . . freedom,] or [an . . . us.] **5.** [He . . . pass,] but [no . . . it.] **6.** [The . . . cut,] but [he . . . stitches.] **7.** [I . . . home,] but [the . . . travel.] **8.** [The . . . over,] and [everyone . . . year.] **9.** [The . . . hardship,] yet [they . . . had.] **10.** [Move . . . here]; [I'll . . . it.] **11.** [Connie . . . football]; [James . . . hockey.] **12.** [I . . . safely,] but [I . . . belts.] **13.** [Please . . . number,] and [I'll . . . work.]

Complex Sentences (P. 40)

A. 1. The shadows [that . . . trees] were a deep purple. **2.** The soldiers waded across the stream [where . . . shallow.] **3.** They waited for me [until . . . came.] **4.** The fans of that team were sad [when the team lost the game.] **5.** [When . . . here,] he was charmed by the beauty of the hills. **6.** Sophia will call for you [when . . . ready.] **7.** Some spiders [that . . . Sumatra] have legs seventeen inches long. **8.** Those [who . . . going] will arrive on time. **9.** Do not throw the bat [after . . . ball.] **10.** Tell us about the trip [that . . . ago.] **B.** Sentences will vary.

Correcting Run-on Sentences (P. 41)

Sentences will vary.

Expanding Sentences (P. 42) A. and B. Sentences will vary.

Unit 2 TEST, Pages 43–44

1. C **2.** B **3.** A **4.** D **5.** C **6.** B **7.** A **8.** A **9.** C **10.** C **11.** B **12.** C **13.** A **14.** C **15.** A **16.** C **17.** B **18.** A **19.** A **20.** B **21.** B **22.** A **23.** A **24.** D **25.** B **26.** C **27.** C **28.** B

Unit 3: Grammar and Usage

Nouns (P. 45)

1. Lupe Garcia; years; supervisor **2.** piece; land; mouth; river, delta **3.** Gilbert Stuart; artist; portraits; presidents **4.** Albert Einstein; scientist; century; Germany **5.** library, world; Alexandria, Egypt **6.** Jim Thorpe; Oklahoma; athletes; world **7.** Mahalia Jackson; singer; spirituals **8.** Marconi; telegraph **9.** parades; games; television; New Year's Day **10.** Terry Fox; runner; leg; cancer; miles; Canada **11.** *Boston News-Letter;* newspaper; United States **12.** message; English Channel; century **13.** Chicago; city; Lake Michigan **14.** seat; window **15.** Kuang; car **16.** children; trip; Carlsbad Caverns **17.** Washington, D.C.; capital; United States **18.** France; food; country; Europe **19.** Maria; car **20.** Hailstones; raindrops; snowflakes **21.** days; summer **22.** rivers, explorers **23.** Jeff; carport; boat **24.** California; home; stars **25.** William Caxton; book; England **26.** Chris; tomatoes; lettuce; cherries; market **27.** building, offices; stores; apartments **28.** Leticia; Peoria; Illinois; friend **29.** airport; hours; snowstorm **30.** pen; ink

Common and Proper Nouns (Pages 46–47)

A. Students should circle the words in bold. **1.** story; prince; pauper; clothing **2. New York; Los Angeles;** cities; **United States 3.** story; **Scrooge; Tiny Tim 4. Sumatra;** island; **Indian Ocean 5. United States;** hail; damage; tornadoes **6.** paper; **Chinese 7. Rikki-tikki-tavi; Rudyard Kipling;** story; mongoose **8.** *Shamrock*; name; emblem; **Ireland 9.** shilling; coin; **England 10.** lights; car; pavement **11. Nathan; Sam; Tuesday 12. Great Sphinx,** monument; **Egypt 13.** family; **Mexico; Canada;** year **B., C., and D.** Answers will vary.

Singular and Plural Nouns (Pages 48–49)

A. 1. brushes **2.** lunches **3.** countries **4.** benches **5.** earrings **6.** calves **7.** pianos **8.** foxes **9.** daisies **10.** potatoes **11.** dishes **12.** stores **B. 1.** booklets **2.** tomatoes **3.** trucks **4.** chefs **5.** branches **6.** toddlers **7.** pennies **8.** potatoes **9.** pieces **10.** doors **11.** islands **12.** countries **13.** houses **14.** garages **15.** fish

16. watches 17. elves 18. desks 19. pans 20. sheep 21. gardens
22. ponies 23. solos 24. trees 25. lights 26. churches 27. cities
28. spoonfuls 29. vacations 30. homes C. 1. apples, oranges,
boxes. 2. letters, friends 3. buildings, elevators 4. families, miles,
lakes 5. tops, cars, storms 6. aunts, uncles

Possessive Nouns (Pages 50–51)
A. 1. brother's 2. boy's 3. Carol's 4. children's 5. grandmother's
6. men's 7. heroes' 8. women's 9. ox's 10. man's 11. Dr. Kahn's
12. soldier's 13. pony's 14. friend's 15. child's 16. engineers'
17. birds' 18. Jon's B. Sentences will vary. C. 1. doctor's
2. senator's 3. sheep's 4. baby's 5. instructor's 6. collectors'
7. spider's 8. Mr. Takata's 9. Tim's 10. Beth's 11. Carl Sandburg's
12. child's 13. women's 14. elephants' 15. sister's 16. Brazil's
17. friends' 18. bird's 19. children's 20. owl's 21. brothers'
22. student's 23. country's 24. owner's 25. uncle's 26. Joan's
27. men's

Appositives (P. 52)
A. Students should circle the words in bold. 1. **Banff**, the large
Canadian national park 2. **painter**, Vincent Van Gogh 3. **The White
House**, home of the President of the United States 4. **Uncle Marco**,
my mother's brother 5. **Earth**, the only inhabited planet in our solar
system 6. **scorpion**, a native of the southwestern part of North
America 7. **cat**, Amelia 8. **Judge Andropov**, the presiding judge
9. **friend**, Luisa B. Answers will vary.

Action Verbs (P. 53)
1. Watch 2. dusted 3. copy 4. burned 5. fell 6. play 7. practiced
8. dashed 9. expresses 10. enjoys 11. leads 12. snowed
13. hiked 14. made 15. hand 16. Draw 17. skated 18. answered
19. repaired 20. suffered 21. Write 22. moved 23. worked
24. directs 25. played 26. walked 27. helped 28. collapsed
29. ticked

Linking Verbs (P. 54)
A. 1. appears 2. is 3. was 4. is 5. looks 6. are 7. smell 8. feels
9. sounds 10. seems B. Answers will vary.

Principal Parts of Verbs (P. 55)
1. is stopping; stopped; (have, has, had) stopped 2. is listening;
listened; (have, has, had) listened 3. is carrying; carried; (have, has,
had) carried 4. is helping; helped; (have, has, had) helped 5. is
starting; started; (have, has, had) started 6. is borrowing;
borrowed; (have, has, had) borrowed 7. is calling; called; (have,
has, had) called 8. is receiving; received; (have, has, had) received
9. is hoping; hoped; (have, has, had) hoped 10. is illustrating;
illustrated; (have, has, had) illustrated 11. is dividing; divided;
(have, has, had) divided 12. is changing; changed; (have, has, had)
changed 13. is scoring; scored; (have, has, had) scored 14. is
ironing; ironed; (have, has, had) ironed 15. is studying; studied;
(have, has, had) studied 16. is collecting; collected; (have, has, had)
collected 17. is laughing; laughed; (have, has, had) laughed

Verb Phrases (P. 56)
A. Sentences will vary. B. 1. has returned 2. has planned 3. would
have answered 4. have been looking 5. have asked 6. have
organized 7. has been planned 8. must speak 9. were dimmed
10. had been seen 11. were threatened 12. are planning

Verb Tenses (P. 57)
A. Answers will vary. B. 1. future 2. past 3. future 4. present
5. past 6. past 7. present 8. future 9. past 10. past

Present Perfect and Past Perfect Tenses (P. 58)
A. 1. past perfect 2. past perfect 3. present perfect 4. past perfect
5. present perfect 6. present perfect 7. present perfect 8. past
perfect 9. present perfect 10. present perfect B. 1. has 2. have
3. had 4. has 5. had 6. has 7. had

Using Is/Are and Was/Were (P. 59)
1. is 2. are 3. is 4. is 5. are 6. is 7. are 8. Are 9. is 10. are
11. were; was 12. were 13. was 14. were 15. were 16. weren't
17. weren't 18. were 19. weren't 20. were 21. was 22. was
23. was 24. Were 25. were 26. Weren't 27. were 28. Were
29. were

Past Tenses of *Give, Take,* and *Write* (P. 60)
A. 1. took 2. taken 3. wrote 4. written 5. gave 6. given 7. written
8. written 9. given 10. wrote 11. taken 12. taken 13. gave
14. took 15. given 16. written 17. took 18. gave 19. written
B. 1. took 2. written 3. gave 4. given 5. taken 6. took 7. gave
8. taken

Past Tenses of *See, Go,* and *Begin* (P. 61)
A. 1. saw 2. gone 3. began 4. went 5. begun 6. seen 7. gone
8. saw 9. seen 10. went 11. begun 12. began 13. gone 14. began
15. begun 16. saw 17. went 18. seen 19. went 20. began
21. began B. Sentences will vary.

Wear, Rise, Steal, Choose, and *Break* (P. 62)
A. 1. worn 2. chosen 3. broke 4. rose 5. stolen 6. chosen 7. worn
8. rose 9. stolen 10. rose 11. worn 12. chose 13. broken
14. stolen 15. risen 16. broken 17. wore 18. risen 19. stole
B. Students should circle the following verbs: had rose, had stole,
worn, chosen, had broke

Come, Ring, Drink, Know, and *Throw* (P. 63)
A. 1. drank 2. rung 3. drunk 4. knew 5. thrown 6. come 7. rang
8. known 9. threw 10. came 11. drunk 12. come 13. knew
14. thrown 15. come 16. rang 17. drank B. Sentences will vary.

Eat, Fall, Draw, Drive, and *Run* (P. 64)
A. 1. drawn 2. driven; began 3. fallen 4. eaten; ran 5. drew 6. run
7. fallen; ran 8. fallen 9. drove 10. eaten 11. ate 12. fallen 13. ran
B. 1. drove 2. drew 3. fallen 4. fell 5. driven 6. ran 7. ate 8. eaten
9. drawn 10. run

Forms of *Do* (P. 65)
A. 1. doesn't 2. did 3. done 4. doesn't 5. did 6. Don't 7. done
8. Don't 9. doesn't 10. don't 11. done 12. did 13. Doesn't
14. Doesn't 15. done 16. doesn't B. and C. Sentences will vary.

Transitive and Intransitive Verbs (P. 66)
A. 1. joined; T 2. wanted; T 3. exercised; I 4. became; I 5. worked;
I 6. preferred; T 7. liked; T 8. switched; I 9. took; T 10. used; T
11. swam; I 12. was; T 13. had; T 14. splashed; I B. Students
should circle the words in bold. 1. walked; **Tiny** 2. pulled; **Carlos**
3. washed; **Tiny** 4. loved; **water** 5. splashed; **Carlos** 6. loved;
bones 7. chewed; **bones** 8. found; **Tiny**

Verbals (Pages 67–68)
A. 1. to quit 2. to finish 3. to run 4. to win 5. to finish 6. to
accomplish 7. to see B. 1. yelling 2. excited 3. running
4. marching 5. Chosen 6. flashing 7. interested C. 1. Studying
2. reading 3. Learning 4. Memorizing 5. Remembering 6. studying
7. Dancing D. 1. infinitive; To act 2. gerund; Acting 3. infinitive; To
write 4. gerund; Working 5. infinitive; to participate 6. participle;
hurried 7. participle; moving 8. infinitive; to read 9. gerund;
Auditioning 10. participle; stirring 11. gerund; Rehearsing
12. infinitive; to memorize 13. participle; convincing 14. gerund;
performing 15. participle; smiling 16. infinitive; To act
17. participle; budding 18. gerund; Performing 19. gerund; Bowing
20. gerund; playing 21. infinitive; To continue 22. gerund; Acting
23. participle; Interrupted 24. gerund; acting 25. infinitive; to excel
26. participle; Well-rehearsed

Active and Passive Voice (P. 69)
A. 1. A 2. A 3. A 4. A 5. P 6. A 7. P 8. P 9. P 10. A
B. and C. Sentences will vary.

Pronouns (Pages 70–71)
A. 1. me 2. them 3. me 4. my 5. he 6. she 7. they 8. us 9. her
10. someone 11. I 12. your 13. He 14. me 15. Who 16. they
17. Everyone 18. their 19. Whom 20. she 21. hers 22. Who
23. ours 24. who B. 1. I; you; him; our 2. Who 3. They; us; we;
their 4. you; me; I; them 5. He; us 6. My; our 7. Whom; you
8. you; me 9. They; us 10. his 11. Who; them 12. She; my; who
13. mine 14. Someone; them 15. Who; she 16. She; us 17. who
18. she; you 19. Who; me 20. we; them 21. Which; your 22. I;
you; our 23. Which; mine 24. you; your 25. you; us 26. anybody
27. You; I 28. you; him C. Sentences will vary.

Antecedents (P. 72)

A. Students should circle the words in bold. **1. Mike**; he **2. Carmen**; her **3. Carmen**; her **4. Mike**; his **5. Carmen**; her; math; it **6. Mike and Carmen**; they **7.** test; it **8.** class; its **9.** palms; they **10. teacher**; he **11.** test; it **12. student**; his or her; test; it **13.** tests; them **14. Carmen**; her **B. 1.** their **2.** him **3.** its **4.** his **5.** they **6.** his **7.** its **8.** their **9.** her **10.** their

Adjectives (P. 73)

A. Adjectives will vary. **B. 1.** This; old; comfortable **2.** a; funny **3.** This; heavy; many; dangerous **4.** The; eager; odd; every **5.** The; tired; thirsty **6.** This; favorite **7.** The; solitary; the; lonely **8.** the; sixth **9.** These; damp **10.** French **11.** those **12.** A; red; the; tall **13.** The; heavy **14.** A; tour; the pirate's **15.** The; gorgeous; Italian **16.** fresh **17.** mashed; baked **18.** Chinese

Demonstrative Adjectives (P. 74)

1. those **2.** That **3.** those **4.** those **5.** That **6.** Those **7.** those **8.** those **9.** these **10.** those **11.** these **12.** these **13.** those **14.** this **15.** Those **16.** these **17.** those **18.** That **19.** These **20.** those **21.** these **22.** these **23.** These **24.** those **25.** Those

Comparing with Adjectives (P. 75)

1. more changeable **2.** most faithful **3.** more agreeable **4.** busiest **5.** longer **6.** loveliest **7.** freshest **8.** higher **9.** more enjoyable **10.** most reckless **11.** youngest **12.** tallest **13.** more difficult **14.** quietest

Adverbs (P. 76)

A. 1. slowly; clearly; expressively **2.** too; recklessly **3.** slowly; quickly **4.** too; harshly **5.** here **6.** everywhere **7.** suddenly; quickly; around **8.** too; rapidly **9.** well **10.** soundly **11.** noisily **12.** early **13.** severely **14.** quickly; steadily **B.** Adverbs will vary.

Comparing with Adverbs (P. 77)

A. 1. sooner **2.** soonest **3.** hard **4.** more **5.** faster **6.** most **B. 1.** fastest **2.** faster **3.** more seriously **4.** most frequently **5.** more quickly **6.** most promptly **7.** more promptly **8.** most eagerly **9.** more carefully **10.** hardest

Prepositions (P. 78)

1. of **2.** of **3.** in **4.** For **5.** At; to; about **6.** of **7.** beside **8.** of **9.** to; at; of **10.** in; in **11.** of; during; of **12.** of; at **13.** at; near **14.** on; for **15.** with **16.** behind **17.** in **18.** of; on; behind **19.** to; during **20.** down **21.** across; in **22.** over; into **23.** of; under **24.** below; of **25.** behind **26.** of; by **27.** between **28.** for

Prepositional Phrases (P. 79)

Students should circle the words in bold. **1.** (above the **clouds**) **2.** (to **North Carolina**) **3.** (on the second **block**) **4.** (on that **hill**) **5.** (on the wet **pavement**) **6.** (in the seventeenth **century**) **7.** (by the **Romans**) **8.** (in **1781**) **9.** (from **Asia**) **10.** (into the **street**) **11.** (in a **pen**) **12.** (over the **fence**) **13.** (in **Denver, Colorado**) **14.** (to **North America**) **15.** (under the **shade**) (of the giant elm **tree**) **16.** (by a scuba **diver**) **17.** (of **soldiers**) (behind the **tank**) **18.** (across the **stream**)? **19.** (across the **nation**) **20.** (into the **sack**) **21.** (up the **pole**) **22.** (in **Nova Scotia**) **23.** (to our **region**) **24.** (in the **Adirondack Mountains**) **25.** (behind a parked **car**)

Prepositional Phrases as Adjectives and Adverbs (P. 80)

1. to the ranch; adverb **2.** in France; adverb **3.** in Tennessee; adjective **4.** to the public library; adverb **5.** in an old house; adverb **6.** with red trim; adjective **7.** in the zoo; adjective **8.** in Burma; adverb **9.** of my money; adjective **10.** over the hat; adverb **11.** of a Sequoia tree trunk; adjective **12.** of New York; adjective **13.** near the docks; adverb **14.** to the movie; adverb **15.** in 1911; adverb **16.** in this room; adjective **17.** across the yard; adverb **18.** of petrified wood; adjective **19.** across the lawn; adverb

Conjunctions (P. 81)

1. whether **2.** and **3.** when **4.** or **5.** and **6.** unless **7.** or **8.** and **9.** and **10.** because **11.** but **12.** and **13.** because **14.** since **15.** but **16.** Although **17.** than **18.** neither/nor **19.** either/or **20.** but **21.** for **22.** while **23.** not only/but also **24.** either/or **25.** neither/nor **26.** Neither/nor

Unit 3 TEST, Pages 82–83

1. B **2.** A **3.** A **4.** B **5.** A **6.** C **7.** A **8.** C **9.** A **10.** A **11.** B **12.** A **13.** B **14.** C **15.** C **16.** A **17.** A **18.** C **19.** C **20.** C **21.** A **22.** A **23.** C **24.** A **25.** D **26.** B **27.** C **28.** A **29.** B **30.** A **31.** B **32.** C **33.** A **34.** C **35.** A **36.** C **37.** A **38.** B **39.** C **40.** C **41.** B **42.** A

Unit 4: Capitalization and Punctuation

Using Capital Letters (Pages 84–86)

Students should circle and capitalize the first letter in each of the following words: **A. 1.** What **2.** Francis; The; Star; Spangled; Banner **3.** Edgar; The; Raven **4.** Paul; When **5.** Who; Snowbound; The; Barefoot; Boy **6.** What; Give **B. 1.** Miami; Florida; Atlanta; Georgia **2.** Potomac; River; Virginia; Maryland **3.** *Pinta*; *Niña*; *Santa*; *María*; Columbus **4.** Spanish; Mississippi; River; English; Jamestown **5.** American; Red; Cross; Clara; Barton **6.** Rocky; Mountains; Andes; Mountains; Alps **C. 1.** Dr.; Thompson **2.** Mayor; Thomas **3.** Dr.; Crawford; W.; Long **4.** Mr.; Mrs.; Randall **5.** Senator; Dixon **6.** Gov.; Alden **7.** Ms.; Howell **D. 1.** Niles School Art Fair/Sat., Feb. 8th, 9 A.M./110 N. Elm Dr. **2.** Shoreville Water Festival/June 23–24/Mirror Lake/Shoreville, MN 55108 **3.** October Fest/October 28 and 29/9 A.M.—5 P.M./63 Maple St. **4.** Barbara Dumont/150 Telson Rd./Markham, Ontario L3R 1E5 **5.** Captain C. J. Neil/*c/o Ocean Star*/P. O. Box 4455/Portsmouth, NH 03801 **6.** Dr. Charles B. Stevens/Elmwood Memorial Hospital/1411 First Street/Tucson, AZ 85062 **E.** Sentences will vary.

Using End Punctuation (Pages 87–88)

A. 1. ? **2.** . **3.** ? **4.** ? **5.** . **6.** . **7.** ? **8.** ? **9.** . **10.** . **11.** ? **12.** . **13.** ? **14.** ? **B. Line 1.** ? **Line 2.** .; . **Line 3.** . **Line 4.** .; . **Line 5.** .; ? **Line 6.** . . **Line 8.** .; . **Line 9.** . . **Line 10.** .; . **Line 11.** . . **Line 12.** .; .; ? **Line 13.** . . **C. 1.** . **2.** . **3.** !; . or ! **4.** !; . **5.** . **6.** . **7.** . or ! **8.** ! **9.** !; !; ! **10.** . **11.** . **12.** ! **13.** ! or . **14.** . **15.** . **16.** ! **17.** . **18.** !; . **D. Line 1.** . . **Line 2.** ! **Line 3.** ?; . **Line 4** . or ! **Line 5.** . . **Line 6.** . . **Line 7.** !; . **Line 8.** . . **Line 9.** . . **Line 10.** ? **Line 11.** .; .

Using Commas (Pages 89–90)

A. 1. Frank, Mary, **2.** anniversary, **3.** with, members, **4.** homes, **5.** active, friendly, **6.** work, **7.** Knudsens, **8.** together, **B. 1.** plans," **2.** said, **3.** said, **4.** asked, **5.** "No, can't," **6.** week," **7.** said, **8.** record," **9.** it," **10.** "Yes, out," **C. 1.** Anthony, a grocery store owner, **2.** "Diane, **3.** "Of course, open," **4.** "Pierre, Elaine's, by," **5.** said, "Stephanie, **6.** "Yes, **7.** asked, "Martin, **8.** "Well, afternoon," **9.** Alan, the butcher, **10.** wait, Alan," **11.** manager, Juan, **12.** "Please, number," **13.** "Yes, usual," **14.** Martin, the produce manager, **15.** Well, **16.** left," **17.** cherries, bananas, **18.** Sara, **19.** cooking, baking, **20.** Today, July 18, **D. Line 1.** Men, women, boys, **Line 2.** event, **Line 3.** games, **Line 4.** track, **Line 5.** swimming, carefully, **Line 6.** challenging, rewarding, **Line 7.** neighbors, Chris Bell, **Line 8.** forget,

Using Quotation Marks and Apostrophes (P. 91)

A. 1. "Wait for me," said Laura, "because . . . you." **2.** "Kim, . . . spacecraft?" asked Tom. **3.** "Where . . . desk?" inquired the stranger. **4.** Joanne asked, "What . . . address?" **5.** David asked, "How . . . Empire?" **6.** "Carlos, . . . article?" asked the teacher. **7.** "Good morning," said Cindy. **8.** Doug asked, "Did . . . fell?" **9.** "The . . . minutes," said Rico. **10.** "Hoan, you're early," said Melissa. **11.** "Come on," said the coach, "you'll . . . game!" **12.** Tony said, "I . . . worker." **B. 1.** didn't; Sue's **2.** Haven't; Paul's **3.** didn't; Tom's **4.** employees'; didn't

Using Colons and Hyphens (P. 92)

A. 1. 2:10 **2.** you: **3.** 4:30 **4.** items: **5.** following: **6.** 8:00; 10:00 **7.** 3:00 **B. 1.** garden-ing **2.** old-fashioned **3.** sign-up **4.** Twenty-seven **5.** daughter-in-law **6.** audi-torium **7.** well-known **8.** long-term

Unit 4 TEST, Pages 93–94

1. A **2.** B **3.** D **4.** C **5.** C **6.** D **7.** D **8.** C **9.** D **10.** A **11.** D **12.** A **13.** B **14.** C **15.** D **16.** C **17.** B **18.** A **19.** C **20.** D **21.** D **22.** A **23.** C **24.** A **25.** B **26.** D **27.** A **28.** C